About Demos

Demos is a greenhouse for new ideas which can improve the quality of our lives. As an independent think tank, we aim to create an open resource of knowledge and learning that operates beyond traditional party politics.

We connect researchers, thinkers and practitioners to an international network of people changing politics. Our ideas regularly influence government policy, but we also work with companies, NGOs, colleges and professional bodies.

Demos knowledge is organised around five themes, which combine to create new perspectives. The themes are democracy, learning, enterprise, quality of life and global change.

But we also understand that thinking by itself is not enough. Demos has helped to initiate a number of practical projects which are delivering real social benefit through the redesign of public services.

We bring together people from a wide range of backgrounds to cross-fertilise ideas and experience. By working with Demos, our partners develop a sharper insight into the way ideas shape society. For Demos, the process is as important as the final product.

www.demos.co.uk

First published in 2004
© Demos
Some rights reserved – see copyright licence for details

ISBN 1 84180 124 0
Typeset by Land & Unwin, Bugbrooke
Printed by Hendy Banks, London

For further information and
subscription details please contact:

Demos
The Mezzanine
Elizabeth House
39 York Road
London SE1 7NQ

telephone: 020 7401 5330
email: hello@demos.co.uk
web: www.demos.co.uk

Disablism

How to tackle the last prejudice

Paul Miller
Sophia Parker
Sarah Gillinson

DEM✪S

i1 6416972

DEMⓒS

Contents

Acknowledgements

This project was made possible by Scope and forms part of their Time To Get Equal campaign. Our sincere thanks to Tony Manwaring who, as well as initiating the project, has been a constant source of encouragement and ideas. We also thank Richard Parnell and Ruth Scott (also at Scope) and Jess Tyrrell at the SMART Company.

Our deep thanks also to Rachel Hurst, director of Disability Awareness in Action, who has been a critical friend throughout the project, always pointing us in the right direction and making it very clear when she thought we'd got it wrong. She has taught us a great deal.

We thank the interviewees whose stories illustrate the report – Katie Caryer, Tara Flood, Clive Gilbert, Toby Hewson, Paul McCarthy, John Quinn and Dean Thomas. Even those who aren't quoted directly influenced our thinking strongly and their ideas and perspectives lie behind much of the piece.

Thanks to Bruce Calderwood, Jane Campbell, Ian Christie, Ian Coates, Neil Crowther, Simon Duffy, David Grayson, Rob Greig, Clare Lombardelli, Julie Mellor, Jenny Morris, Jeremy Myerson, Kate Oakley, Andy Rickell, Liz Sayce, Susan Scott-Parker and James Strachan, who all provided invaluable input and comments or allowed us to interview them about specific areas of policy or practice.

Thanks also to all those who attended Scope's National Forum and helped sharpen the argument in the latter stages of the project.

At Demos, Tom Bentley, Eddie Gibb, Helen McCarthy, Paul Skidmore and James Wilsdon have provided support and advice with their usual good humour and insight. Bobby Webster masterminded the production process.

As ever though, all errors and omissions remain our own.

Paul Miller, Sophia Parker and Sarah Gillinson
May 2004

Disablism *n.* discriminatory, oppressive or abusive behaviour arising from the belief that disabled people are inferior to others.

(although you won't find a definition in a dictionary)

Foreword

Rachel Hurst and Tony Manwaring

That we are writing a joint foreword to this report is a story in itself – this collaboration between a disabled person with a long history as a leader of the disability rights movement and a non-disabled person recently appointed as chief executive of one of the large disability charities is significant.

What unites us is actually very simple. It is a shared view: that disabled people in this country lead lives that are blighted by poverty and exclusion; that disabled people are much less likely than non-disabled people to be able to achieve their potential; and that the hard fought for and won advances that disabled people and their families have secured cannot be taken for granted, and are anyway not nearly enough. We think it is worth seeing whether we can help to bring about change by working together – alongside all the other relationships that we each have – and by working with Demos.

We are exploring the possibilities of collaboration because we recognise the need to come to terms with the limitations of working on our own when dealing with the scale of the social change that is so urgently required to confront the extent and impact of the disablism that we face. We believe that this Demos report is the first contribution to mainstream debate on disability issues that recognises the existence and threat of disablism in this country.

Disablism casts a shadow over the emerging areas of policy that will shape society in the future, and exists, for example, in the attitudes and responses to genetic advances and the promotion of eugenic solutions in many bioethical situations. There is no political commitment to eradicate institutional disablism and disabled people's rights as citizens and human beings are not sufficiently advanced by the prevailing political climate. Although there have been some important and practical advances, the rights of disabled people are far too low on the policy and social agendas at the level of European, national and local government.

Disablism exists in the under-resourcing of and low status accorded to disabled people and their organisations; they are left off the policy-making agenda. In all areas of social and political life disabled people are typically seen as persons requiring charity and services, not as human beings with full civil rights. They are all too often objects of pity and compassion. And yet disabled people are people whose difference should be celebrated, whose contribution to society as people of integrity and perseverance should be appreciated, and whose right to determine the key decisions that shape their own lives should always be enabled and paramount.

The disability rights movement has much to celebrate – as recognised in this Demos report. The movement has been a powerful advocate for legislative change, and has moved the rights of disabled people further up the agenda than would ever otherwise have been possible. Above all, the disability rights movement is made up of and led by disabled people who seek to determine the future of disabled people in this country. Any collaboration and movement for further change must build on this and strengthen the position of disabled people as leaders.

As with racism and sexism, disablism is the concern of everybody – and everybody needs to be involved in its eradication. Therefore the disability rights movement is unlikely to achieve the scale of change that is required to achieve a 'step change' in the lives of disabled people in this country on its own. Such a step change will, logically, require a fundamental shift in attitudes and culture in British society, underpinned by law, rooted in the human and civil rights of disabled people. To achieve this it will be necessary to build a movement for change – one that finds sufficient common ground between disabled and non-disabled people, between the rights movement and disability charities, and between disability organisations and government, employers and other key stakeholders.

Individual stakeholders cannot hope to bring this scale of change about on their own; together we might stand a chance. But seeing whether this is possible or not is fraught with difficulty. The disability world is hugely under-resourced and undervalued; trust is at a premium, often for good reason. The experience and in some cases the practice of working with disability charities has been problematic, to say the least.

Government alone cannot effect such change, though it can do much to support it. Companies can similarly reinforce and underpin this process for change, but – as employers and providers of goods and services – it would go beyond their function and purpose to play a more proactive and catalytic role. So we need to move things forward, one step at a time. But each step that we take should be informed by a broader vision of the change in society that we want to bring about.

Scope, at least, needs to change to ensure that we model equality and therefore practise what we preach. Scope is taking a root and branch look at what we do and how we do it. The 'Diversity Works' initiative has been launched to increase the numbers of disabled people employed within Scope and beyond. A set of standards is being developed so that disabled people who are service users can assess the extent to which Scope services promote decisions based on principles of independence and choice. Campaign networks have been formed and are being developed that allow disabled people to shape Scope's campaigning priorities and activities. Scope's strategic and corporate priorities will increasingly be shaped by the key issues and barriers faced by disabled people, building on Scope's governance; a majority of trustees are disabled people.

Over the last few months Scope and Disability Awareness in Action (DAA) have been exploring the opportunity for dialogue and for joint working with others in the disability rights movement – the result is that we have together produced a 'statement for collaboration', see page 17. We are sharing it now to provide an example and perhaps a framework within which thinking about the value of these tactics and this approach could take place. This statement is the work of all concerned, and over the months to come we will see whether this statement can be useful and whether others will put their names to it.

The statement of collaboration is also a practical example of the concept developed in the Demos report of 'trading zones'. When this idea was first developed we were sceptical about it but we have become converts. If collaboration is important we also need ground rules for collaboration to have any chance of success. Trading zones are powerful because they create a framework within which each participant in that zone is able to contribute equally, to share views and come to a common position.

Within the statement there is a recognition that we will each do what we have done as before, but we will also see whether other, more overarching, objectives can be better achieved together. We will have to work out what the 'deal' is, find ways of collaborating and identify what changes are needed to build trust. But the statement also addresses tougher subjects. For example, some sections of the disability rights movement should be prepared to work in partnership with organisations like Scope – at least on specific projects and activities that are of mutual benefit – and not then be critical of the results of the collaboration at each and every opportunity! And Scope, at least, must review what it does and how it does it rigorously on the basis of shared principles to find the best way to model equality in practice; in doing so it needs to work out how the resources it has can be shared appropriately and used by others in the movement.

This report is set in the context of the Time To Get Equal campaign that Scope is launching, with substantial input from individuals within the disability movement. We want this campaign to raise awareness, to challenge thinking and perceptions, and to become a vehicle that disabled people and others committed to the rights of disabled people can support. Although we will continue to argue for changes in the law, this campaign acknowledges that they will not be enough on their own – we need to challenge attitudes, to support and empower disabled people, and to create new cultures.

Above all, we need to confront disablism. The scale and magnitude of the disablism that exists in our society and our institutions, and the effect it has, makes it necessary for us to look at new ways of working. Some may feel uncomfortable with the term disablism. Why talk about another 'ism'? The facts speak for themselves. As this report shows, when you start to look at the lives of disabled Britons you have to draw the conclusion that disablism exists. And if you do not name that which has to be defeated, it will not be beaten.

Women have fought and lost their lives in the cause of equality, and even today substantial inequalities still exist on the basis of gender. It has taken a number of high profile and shocking cases to force through the realisation that institutional racism exists and must be confronted. But at least there is now an acceptance that discrimination on the grounds of gender and race has no place in a modern society. There is no such acceptance in relation to disablism.

Through collecting evidence from newspapers and law reports, DAA has recorded on its 'violations database' that since 1990 in this country 682 disabled people have lost their lives because of disablism. That is, they have been deliberately killed just because they were a disabled person. Their deaths were the result of hate crimes, mercy killings, fear, prejudice and the costs of health care. Those women and black people who have lost their lives are known – nobody knows of these 682 disabled people.

Finally, a word on why we commissioned Demos to produce this report. Demos has won a reputation for producing interesting and thought-provoking interventions on issues of policy and strategy, which are taken seriously by government, opinion formers and decision-makers in big companies – in short, by those with the power to affect people's lives. Discussions on the inclusion of disabled people and accessibility for them are too important to be left to the margins of politics: they should be in the mainstream, where they are far more likely to be treated seriously and to initiate decision-making that will improve the lives of disabled people. So working with Demos provides a new possibility of seeking to bring about change.

This report will not change the world, but we hope it will challenge the way people think and the way government behaves and makes decisions. We look forward to more and more people, especially those who are in positions of power and influence, coming to an understanding that there is such a thing as disablism, acknowledging their role in perpetuating it and recognising the part that we can all play to eradicate it.

In years to come we want to be part of a society that has tackled disablism and fundamentally advanced the human and civil rights of disabled people. We believe that this report, the campaign of which it is part and the dialogue for collaboration without which it would not have been produced can make an important contribution to bringing this about.

Rachel Hurst is director of Disability Awareness in Action;
Tony Manwaring is chief executive of Scope.

THE HUMAN AND CIVIL RIGHTS OF DISABLED PEOPLE: STATEMENT OF COLLABORATION

Sharing a common anger at this situation, and acknowledging that we are all working within our own spheres to effect social change, we believe that it is important to grasp an opportunity to work together to:

- find collaborative solutions to ensuring disability rights are pushed further up the political and social agendas, and mainstreamed within national and local policy
- challenge the barriers faced by disabled Britons
- explore the potential for new partnerships.

We are united in wishing an end to institutional disablism and the enforced segregation of disabled people.

We are all committed to the full and equal participation of disabled people as citizens of the UK.

We acknowledge that we are coming to this unity and commitment from different perspectives and agree to observe the dignity and expertise of each of us equally. We recognise that our diversity offers a source of real strength.

However, we acknowledge that the voice of disabled people themselves has, traditionally, been left out of planning policies and programmes that directly affect them.

Therefore we believe that this voice must be positively supported and should provide a leading role in our collaboration.

We also acknowledge that, historically, there has been an unfair distribution of resources – and the resulting power structures – between the disability rights movement and the large charitable disability organisations.

Therefore we will take that imbalance into consideration.

We are therefore committed to collaborating, because we believe that working together we *must* achieve more to advance our common goal – that disabled people achieve the full human and civil rights that should be enjoyed by all Britons, irrespective of difference.

1. Stories of disablism

The barriers facing disabled people today

Disablism blights our society. From getting an education to getting around, building a career to becoming a parent, going out with friends to using the internet, disabled people face many more challenges than their non-disabled fellow citizens and are routinely discriminated against and excluded. Nobody could seriously suggest that disabled people *should* have fewer opportunities than non-disabled people but somehow we find ourselves in a situation where the reality, as lived by disabled people today, would suggest otherwise.

* * *

Take Katie Caryer. She wants to 'change the world'. She loves doing drama like so many young people. But where most non-disabled people have the luxury of being their own greatest barrier to achieving these things, the same is not true for Katie. When she travels alone on the bus, people have been known to call the police, believing she's 'escaped' from an institution or shouldn't be out alone. At school, she felt 'like the little green man with 1,000 kids' surrounding her – 'no one sat next to me because I drool, but teacher says, "good kids, keep going on"'. To Katie and her family it felt as if some of the teachers at the school were trying to prove a point: that someone like Katie shouldn't be in mainstream education. Katie's adamant that she should have been.

The barriers Katie faces don't just make things difficult, they often make them impossible. But she knows there's no reason it has to be this way. Katie has had experiences which show how education, friendship and independent living might be. She has taken part in workshops at the Chicken Shed Theatre which she describes as being 'like an opposite world' from secondary school which was 'just awful'. She loves the university where she's now studying performing arts and finds herself 'not a bit under-average…but a bit over-average'.

Katie is passionate about getting personal assistants for disabled people who need them – she believes that would make a massive difference to some people's lives and has set up a campaign with a group of other disabled people to make sure the message gets heard.

* * *

Rob Taylor (not his real name) is a civil servant and he's under no illusions that all managers in the civil service treat disabled people equally. 'A lot of the time people aren't intending to put disabled people down,' he said, 'but a manager once put in my appraisal that I was "cheerful". Fine, I thought, but I want to know how well I'm doing!' He's seen and heard of a lot of instances of discrimination against disabled people in the civil service and although edicts from on high say that they should be treated equally, it isn't the case everywhere. As he put it, 'The fact that you have guidelines in a personnel handbook is one thing but in reality, every department, every site is different.'

Disabled people are aware of these differences and will avoid departments and specific offices that have a bad reputation. 'No matter how many slick-looking documents you produce, unless you address the working experience of disabled people, you'll develop a reputation very quickly that says "look elsewhere".' The prejudice isn't just bad for the individual concerned, it matters for the Civil Service as a whole. As Rob says, 'I've got no doubt that there are disabled people working in the civil service whose skills are not being fully used because of the prejudices of people above them…. It's perceived as being disadvantageous to declare your disability…. People have preconceptions like "they'll be wanting time off to go for doctor's appointments".'

Rob acknowledges that the system with all its bureaucracy and procedure doesn't always help: 'If I want an easy life am I really going to hire someone who's declared a disability?' There are no easy answers to achieving equality – '[It] is an ongoing process, not something that's done when a box is ticked!'

* * *

Tara Flood is a gold-medal-winning Paralympic swimmer, but when she was younger she 'felt like a fish out of water in the real world'. She worked for a bank until the level of discrimination, both obvious and more subtle, convinced her it was time to leave. There were a number of examples: 'One time I wanted to move to a different department, and I was told that I might not be the right image for the bank. There were many times that I was not allowed into client meetings – even though I was a team leader and always spoke to them on the phone. And I wasn't getting promotions.'

When Tara was two she was sent to a special school and feels very strongly that the segregated education has had a lasting negative impact on her relationship with her family, her educational opportunities and, for many years after she left school, on the way she viewed herself.

> *We were told that we must be as 'normal' as possible. The big shock was leaving school and finding I was on my own and having to communicate with non-disabled people. I had no idea what to say to them. So I spent the next ten years in the disability closet. People didn't ask about my impairment, and I worked so hard to pretend it didn't exist. It was like the elephant in the room that no one wants to talk about…. So although I challenged some of the bank's decisions, I never did it on the*

basis of my impairment. I just didn't want that discussion. I suppose I felt that if I admitted that I am disabled, they would see it, and it would become overt. It was entirely irrational, like a secret you don't want anyone to know and everyone was part of the conspiracy.

It was when Tara 'woke up' to the social model of disability that things changed. The social model gives disabled people the chance to realise that they personally aren't the problem. The problem (or 'mess' as we'll describe it more accurately later) is in the systems that do not allow disabled people to participate as full members of society. That Mike Oliver (an academic who has written about the social model) features in the BBC's top ten 'Greatest Disabled Britons' tells us something about its importance for disabled people.[1]

'I had a sudden realisation that everything that's happened was because of how people look at impairment – as different, less, unacceptable…. Suddenly you can be the person you always thought you were but never could be.' Now Tara is a campaigner rallying other disabled people to realise that the problem isn't with them but with the society that holds them back.

* * *

The first school photograph on the mantelpiece has pride of place in the living room of Dean Thomas's flat in Nottingham. We asked what life was like for disabled parents. Dean sighed and then said, 'very difficult'. Dean has a son who is five years old and because of his experience of becoming a father got involved in a network for disabled people who are parents or considering becoming parents.

He tells us, 'Disabled parents are quite often scared to ask for support. They're afraid it will end up as a child protection issue.' Even if they do ask, the usual support systems aren't used to working with disabled parents. 'Very few local authorities are geared up to deal with disabled parents properly so it falls on volunteers to provide support.' This is despite the often simple nature of their requests: 'You get disabled people who can look after themselves but need a little bit of extra support in their parenting responsibilities.'

A quick institutional fix won't be enough though – the issue is more deeply embedded in people's attitudes. As Dean comments, 'It just doesn't fit neatly into people's psyches that disabled people can or should become parents. Although I'm sure you'd find that statistically they make a better job of it.'

Systemic disablism

These few stories are just the beginning. Every disabled person has been subject to some kind of barrier or discrimination that a non-disabled person would not have to face. As Len Barton has put it, 'To be disabled means to be discriminated against.'[2] Looking at the more macro statistics, the picture doesn't look any rosier. These are just a small selection:[3]

- O   In summer 2003, only 49 per cent of disabled people of working age were in work, compared with 81 per cent of non-disabled people in work.[4]
- O   By the time they are 30, one in three (30 per cent) disabled people in a recent survey expected to be earning less than other people their age.[5]
- O   Recent figures show that the proportion of disabled senior civil servants has remained almost static since 1998, now standing at 1.7 per cent, and looks unlikely to reach the government's own target of 3 per cent by 2005.[6]
- O   Overall, seven in ten (73 per cent) of disabled people with mobility and sensory impairments in Great Britain said they have difficulty accessing goods and services. The main difficulty reported by respondents was gaining physical access to premises.[7]
- O   Of the thousand public websites tested by City University's Centre for Human Computer Interaction Design, 81 per cent failed to meet the basic accessibility criteria laid down by the Web Accessibility Initiative.[8]

○ Even if public transport is accessible (most still isn't), disabled people are almost twice as likely as non-disabled people to say that they are fearful of travelling on it, and many consider the private car to be the only form of transport that is convenient and accessible.[9]

○ Only 0.5 per cent of people aged between 16 and 24 who had some sort of physical impairment were accepted by UCAS for a place at university. This compares with about 8 per cent of the same age group who had no health problem.[10]

○ Just two of Britain's 21 national newspapers say they employ disabled journalists, according to a survey in *Disability Now*.[11]

○ Disabled people are more worried than non-disabled people about crime – the percentage of disabled people who feel frightened going out after dark is more than double that of non-disabled people.[12]

○ 22 per cent of disabled respondents in a recent survey have experienced harassment in public in relation to their impairment.[13]

Furthermore, documented evidence collected by Disability Awareness in Action on its database of violations against disabled people shows that since 1990 thousands of disabled people have suffered degrading and inhuman treatment – verbal, sexual and physical abuse – and hundreds more have been killed, murdered or denied life-saving treatment.

The point is – it shouldn't be like this.

Looking back to look ahead

The postwar period saw the birth of two great changes, which have affected the way disability is treated today: the modern welfare state and the human and civil rights movements. Welfare created support, which enshrined social equality as a legitimate public goal; universal rights created the basis for empowerment movements and anti-discrimination laws.

These histories have left a legacy – not just a set of institutions that promote fairness in particular ways, but a set of assumptions about how to bring about positive social change. We know that discrimination is sustained and reproduced at every level of society, but we almost always look to laws and governments to fix it. We know that our society is becoming more diverse and fluid, yet campaigners often seek general rules and powers to make it fair. We know that, more and more, all people want an active part in shaping their own life, yet we blame remote institutions and political leaders for not giving it to us.

The civil rights movements born in the 1960s took fresh claims to fairness from the framework implied by human rights – the equal worth of each person – and allied them with the moral energy and radicalism of social movements. Disability, as we will see, took longer to reach the top of the legislative agenda in the UK, and its leading campaigners have had to fight hard to be recognised. Historically, social movements take the claims of particular groups and make their case impossible for the majority to ignore. Protection through law is therefore the ultimate form of recognition, a sign that the issues have influenced the political mainstream. But though law may be a precondition of justice it cannot always guarantee that change will flow through to the everyday reality of people's perceptions and behaviour.

Most of us agree that multiple actions are needed to achieve lasting social change, but our institutions are designed to privilege legal rules and executive powers over other, more diffuse processes. The result may be that we have a framework of legislation designed to protect rights, but that equally necessary cultural change is yet to come. Given the subtlety and pervasiveness of the issues, and the diversity of personal solutions, enforcing the law may be a blunt instrument.

So how should we now go about approaching disablism? Disability is complex and one size fits all policies are no more applicable to disabled people than they are to the population at large. Although there's a tendency to think of disabled people as wheelchair users, in reality 'disability' covers a whole range of impairments, and wheelchair users make up a small percentage of disabled people. Indeed there's no such thing as an 'average' disabled person. Some people have conditions that come and go. Some impairments can be invisible – and the adjustments that are needed more subtle. Some people have multiple impairments; some people's impairments are more severe than others'. And it's not just that 'disability' covers a range of impairments; disabled people also have a diverse range of opinions and identities. Some disabled people identify themselves as disabled, some don't, some do some of the time. What they have in common is the barriers and prejudice they face – or, in one word, disablism.

While there are, and will be, substantial benefits from medical research and the new genetic sciences, technical progress in this area can carry new, subtle, but pervasive, forms of discrimination against disabled people. One example is the rationing of health care services in relation to quality of life assessments. These assessments all too frequently undervalue disabled people's lives and treatment is not considered worth giving. Genetic-based solutions, either in terms of prenatal detection, termination or cure, may appear attractive to many people fearful of the consequences of having to care for a disabled child or adult in an uncaring and unsupportive society. However, these solutions reinforce the supposed negative consequences of disabling impairments, ignoring the important contribution disabled people can make as part of a diverse society. At their worst, such solutions make judgements about the value of a disabled person's life itself.

We can't put 'disability policy' in a neat box, either. There is a multitude of organisations who have a stake in or who make decisions that affect the lives of disabled people. All of these organisations have their own slant on how best to serve disabled people and how the system should work. Put together they constitute a complex, often unfathomable system, which can be very difficult to navigate.

The disability lobby has a reputation within Westminster and Whitehall as a formidable and angry opponent. From high-level lobbying to protesters chained to railings their relentless efforts have led to significant victories (although some within the movement might argue about how good each piece of legislation is):

- The final phase of the Disability Discrimination Act 1995 (DDA), which requires service providers to look at making reasonable adjustments to physical barriers, comes into force in October 2004.
- The positive duty to promote equality in relation to disabled people will also come into force in 2004, giving public bodies similar requirements to those under the Race Relations (Amendment) Act 2000.
- In 2000 the Disability Rights Commission (DRC) was established as an independent voice for disabled people.
- The Special Educational Needs and Disability Act 2001 (SENDA) makes it unlawful to discriminate against disabled people seeking access to education.

In addition, the Human Rights Act 1998 ensures the right of each individual person born or living in the UK to life, freedom and dignity, and ensures their protection against discrimination in the promotion of all those rights. The Criminal Justice Act 2003 protects disabled people from harassment and abuse. Together they confirm disabled people as citizens of the UK and their right to consideration as human beings.

But legislation is only a start and compared with other equality agendas disability is behind the game. As the stories and statistics illustrate there is a long way to go before equality is achieved. While the legislation is on a par with that for race or gender equality, the lived experience of disabled people is still extremely poor because of disablism.

Disabled people are a growing group. The demographic shift taking place in Europe and North America towards an ageing population means that more and more people are covered by the definition of 'disabled' under the DDA. In 2003, 10 per cent of 16 to 24-year-olds were disabled while this proportion increases to one-third in the 50 to retirement age category.[14] In many ways non-disabled people are not-yet-disabled people. Politicians should be running the numbers. Disabled people constitute a growing group in electoral terms, both in terms of their numbers and in the volume of their voice. To put it bluntly: if things were tight, disabled people could sway an election.

A note about language

Language is important in all equality agendas, and disability is no different. This report uses the terms 'disability' and 'impairment' quite separately.

Most people have an impairment, however minor – but they are not disabled unless there is a negative social response to them because of the impairment. For instance, a person with impaired vision requiring reading glasses would not see themselves as disabled if they lived in the UK. But if they lived in a rural area of Africa they may well be, as they might have been excluded from a proper education and would find it more difficult to find employment.

Disability describes how society responds to people with impairments; it is not a description of a personal characteristic. A disabled person is not a 'person with a disability' as the person does not own the disability in the way that you might be 'a person with brown hair'. The opposite of disabled is not able-bodied or abled – it is non-disabled or enabled.

We also use the term 'disablism' in this report. Unlike sexism or racism, you won't find disablism in the dictionary. Yet it describes an all-too-real issue: discriminatory, oppressive or abusive behaviour arising from the belief that disabled people are inferior to others. 'Institutional disablism' describes a whole organisation's disablist attitudes, practice and culture.

This report

This report is not about looking at the statistics and trying to solve inequalities one by one. Nor is it about looking from the top down at how to reform existing institutions or legislation now in place. Instead, we take the lived experience of disabled people as our starting point. We consider how reconfiguration of the relationships between some of these organisations, and changing the characteristics of the spaces in which those relationships take place, might help.

Four years ago Demos published the pamphlet *An Inclusive Future?*, which was the result of a year-long research project commissioned by the National Disability Council.[15] This report builds on that analysis. It isn't just about *why* we should be tackling the challenges that disabled people face in almost everything they do. It's about *how* those challenges can be overcome, suggesting that focusing on the impairment might not be the best way forward. In other words it's less about what disabled people can't do, and more about what they can do, in many cases far better than non-disabled people.

Disablism is based on a series of interviews with disabled people that took place in March 2004 across the UK. We also conducted interviews with a number of people from government departments, disability organisations and some people outside the field of 'disability policy' who we thought might be able to offer a fresh perspective. Early on in the process we created a set of 15 working propositions, which we posted on the Demos website and sent out through our networks. We received a great deal of valuable feedback and this is a process we intend to repeat on other projects.

There are two core stories that lie at the heart of this report. First, a story about the challenge that disablism presents to everyone, and the importance – again, for everyone – of overcoming this challenge. The second story is about change and how it happens. Over the course of the next three chapters we will argue that:

○   the lived experience of disabled people presents a
    powerful critique to the current way in which the
    government understands 'work' and 'support'; to bring
    about meaningful and positive change, it is critical that we
    start in the right place – in other words, with the needs
    and aspirations of individuals

○ disabled people must be involved in the processes of product and service innovation if their needs are to be responded to; inclusive design and participatory processes offer an approach to innovation that will benefit everyone, and disabled people have the potential to lead the way

○ disablism is as much about changing attitudes as it is about reforming services and products; networked campaigning, rather than top-down change, offers a new and powerful way of understanding the roles and responsibilities that key players in the change process will need to take in the future.

Service providers in the public, private and voluntary sectors are wrestling with the challenge of making their services more personalised and responsive to users' needs. Overall, politics is suffering a crisis of disengagement and legitimacy. People are increasingly rejecting conventional models and methods for bringing about change, but simultaneously demand a greater say in how their lives are run.

On the historical model, the struggle to achieve fairness for disabled people would follow the cycle of wider social change. That is, the new expectations for everyday life would become the focus of campaigning and public policies designed to help disabled people 'catch up' and to have their complex needs recognised. But a vision of complex equality in a personalised, fluid society must be able to harness the changes affecting everyone. As we will argue, disabled people are not only entitled to be at the forefront of wider public change; they have distinctive contributions to make which could help improve everybody's quality of life. As trailblazers of more personalised support systems and a more direct engagement in social development and innovation, the participants in this change could be helping to shape a new politics of engagement and shared ownership.

Achieving all of this will rely on choreographing different components of change so that they occur simultaneously and deliver a cumulative impact. This approach stands in contrast with the assumption that legislation is enough on its own to trigger ongoing social, organisational or cultural change. This will mean asking questions about how change happens, and the best ways for those with a stake in disability to work with others to achieve results over time. Our overarching proposal is that new 'trading zones', created in the spaces between existing institutions and expectations, could accelerate the process of change by generating innovations that can spread more widely across society, and by creating working models of collaborative participation that exemplify the contribution that all of us could make to overcoming the barriers of disablism. In the next chapter we turn to this idea of trading zones: why they are needed, and what they involve.

2. Lost in translation
The importance of 'trading zones'

It started with a barbecue, good food and warm weather making the conversation that little bit easier. Back in 1981, 250 disabled people were at a large conference of 3,000 people organised by Rehabilitation International. The barbecue, however, was hosted by the Canadian Coalition of Disabled People in honour of the disabled people from all around the world who had arrived in Canada for the conference. What made it a significant evening was the fact that, for the first time, these people found out that there were alarming commonalities in how they experienced their societies. The exclusion and abuses that many of them had put down to their own locale in fact cut across cultures, countries and indeed continents. A shared unity of purpose emerged.

They asked the organisers at Rehabilitation International why they had no real voice in the larger conference's programme, and why disabled people only numbered 250 in a conference of 3,000 people. When they were denied a substantive voice in the programme they decided to abandon it in favour of their own workshops and planning sessions. Ultimately they decided to form an international organisation of disabled people, with the objective being the full and equal participation of disabled people in society, and comprehensive implementation of their rights. Disabled Peoples' International (DPI) was born.[16]

The story illustrates a common occurrence in circumstances where disabled people feel they have been excluded from decision-making –

a gap opening up between them and the institution in question and an atmosphere of antagonism developing in the relationship. In choosing to leave the conference and set up their own workshops, the group of people who came to represent DPI challenged Rehabilitation International's modus operandi. And as a starting point they argued that change would never come about unless disabled people were able to represent themselves rather than be spoken for.

For some people in the disability movement change requires direct action. For others, without legislation true change will never happen. For others still, change is about cultures rather than structures and it is attitudes that will lead the way to the future. There is little agreement across the movement or between the movement and government and other actors about which are the key elements or drivers that will bring about change for the better. And just to make things even worse, this lack of clarity about how change happens leads to a confusion about the roles and responsibilities different people should take. Without a shared script for describing the process of change, no one is clear what part they play.

This is compounded by the fact that people have multiple perspectives on what it is that needs to change: there is not a shared understanding of what the problems are. One person's devastating critique of the issues might be complete nonsense for another person. We all make sense of the world differently and use different frameworks to understand the nature of the problems and challenges we face. There cannot be an 'objective' viewpoint when the questions being dealt with are about human experience and social problems, and the sooner this is recognised the better. Nonetheless, for lasting public change to take place and be accepted, shared perspectives do need to emerge. This tension between shared understanding and personal experience is one factor that makes disability issues extremely complex.

A lot of metaphorical shouting has gone on between the various groups involved in the disability debate. When one group's point of view hasn't been accepted by the opposite side (sometimes even thought of as the enemy), the temptation has been to say the same thing, only louder. The problem is that each group involved has a different set of assumptions, experiences and insights, which together mean that that group's culture is distinct. For example, as DPI has developed its members have created a set of terms and acronyms of their own, aspects of a language for discussing the issues with each other. The same is true of individual government departments, each of which has a set of Three Letter Acronyms (TLAs) and shorthands of their own. This is perfectly normal and understandable – it helps organisations and groups to work effectively within their own boundaries. The problem comes when these cultures meet and things get lost in translation.

Difficulties and messes

We are, quite literally, in a mess when it comes to understanding how change can happen when thinking about disability issues, as we are in thinking about race, gender and other equality agendas. The methodology of systems thinking can perhaps help to untangle some of these problems. Jake Chapman has argued that broadly speaking there are two types of problem: 'difficulties' and 'messes'.[17] A difficult problem might be how to get a man on the moon. A messy problem might be how to bring up a child in the best possible way. In a mess, unlike a difficulty, there is little clarity or agreement about what a solution would look like, or how it would be achieved, or indeed when you've reached that solution; equally the relationship between cause and effect is often non-linear and uncertain. A mess is unbounded in time, scope or resources.

Disability debates are, by this definition, messes rather than difficulties. Systems approaches argue that messes cannot be rationalised, compartmentalised or simplified into policy silos. The idea of command and control, of determining the inputs necessary to achieve the desired outputs, makes no sense when talking about messes. The analogy that has been made by renowned systems thinker Paul Pslek is of that between throwing a rock and throwing a bird. Newtonian physics can predict the trajectory of the rock, based on calculations about the way it was thrown, where it was thrown from and so on. However, it would struggle to predict with any accuracy the trajectory of the bird. Messy problems – with a lack of clarity about what the solution is, and indeed what the problem was in the first place – are more like birds.

It is ironic in this context that the one agenda that can truly be seen as shared between government and the disability movement is the need for top-down, directive legislation and initiatives. Tom Bentley has argued:

> *Command and control is a framework unsuited to the complex, unpredictable demands of contemporary organisational life.... [Command and control frameworks] assume a directive model of institutional authority in which the priorities, values and knowledge held at the centre of an institution or community will shape and control the behaviour of those who make up the wider system.*[18]

If disability is a messy problem, with multiple perspectives and multiple drivers for change, solutions can never emerge solely from a command and control framework. While legislation is important, we need to find ways of understanding change that can take account of the different interests and experiences of people, whether they are approaching matters as a disabled person, a policy-maker, an employee or a parent. We have to learn how to work together and to recognise and make use of the different ways of seeing. This is likely to require a plan of action that operates at a number of levels. The truth is that no one person, group or institution is either solely to blame or has the magic solution to inequality.

This doesn't simply mean we make another plea for 'holistic' government. Too often the aspiration of 'joined-up' government has been described without any analysis of how we might achieve it. Instead, as this report will argue, the key to bringing about sustainable and meaningful change lies with focusing on the characteristics of the *interactions between* different actors in the debate. If we're to move forward in enabling disabled people to achieve their full potential, all those groups with a stake in achieving that change will need to rethink their roles in relation to other groups and particularly the ways in which they communicate and collaborate.

Systems thinking emphasises the influence of 'feedback loops' on people and organisations. The history of disability debates suggests that the framing of the issues has a powerful effect on the working relationships created around them. A history of neglect, disrespect and deep-seated disablism has, in the past, created a situation where attention-seeking and oppositional strategies have been necessary to confront the issues and get them acknowledged. But such strategies often lead to reactive institutional responses, which create new categories of activity to deal with the claims of a particular constituency – new policy responsibilities, directives or regulations. This way of defining responsibilities in turn sets up specialised and often antagonistic relationships, mapping out 'territory' for different groups to occupy across the issues, but doing little to integrate what is being learned about solutions into other areas of society.

It may be that change in the gaps between the institutions and organisations is more important than change in the organisations themselves. It is here we can introduce the idea of 'trading zones' – a concept originating from the history of science literature – as a means of refocusing in this way. It's an idea we will return to throughout the report and we'll propose specific ways that trading zones could and should be established and reconfigured in the final chapter.

Lessons from the lab

In some ways it's amazing that anything happens in science at all as there has always been a problem of miscommunication and snobbery. Physicists thinking of engineers as grimy-handed thugs using cut corner techniques, chemists thinking of physicists as impractical dreamers, and so on. That's before the scientists come face to face with any government administrators who might have an interest in the project. Each group has a very strong culture of its own: a literature, a set of jargon and acronyms that are often totally impenetrable to outsiders. Sometimes they're even impenetrable to insiders. They have different worldviews, different sets of techniques for problem solving.

Of course this is why getting them to work together is so valuable. While no one person knows the techniques of every discipline or sub-discipline, if they can communicate and collaborate with people from other disciplines it's possible to draw on other perspectives when necessary. Sometimes, by bringing together very different people, amazing things happen.

This is the significance of the 'trading zones': where people from (in this case) different academic disciplines or different branches of the same discipline (say the experimentalists and the theorists) interact to solve problems. As Harvard Professor Peter Galison who coined the term explains, 'My concern is with the site – partly symbolic and partly spatial – at which the local coordination between beliefs and action takes place. It is a domain I call the trading zone.'[19]

The 'trading' metaphor shouldn't be thought of in shopping mall terms. It supposes equal exchange, rather than a consumer-based understanding of commerce where people are often excluded by virtue of their income or status. It is a place where people come together bringing with them something of value, be that resources, skills, experience or ideas, and after exchange and interaction leave with something of benefit.

Our proposition is that when this analysis is transferred to the disability arena these desirable characteristics have often been absent in the interactions over policy that have most affected the ability of disabled people to achieve their full potential. This needs to change.

Getting into the zone

While specific policy measures and changes inside the structures that support disabled people are important, to achieve the kinds of step change necessary, new relationships and reconfigurations of existing ones will be vital. Trading zones are an attempt to create some sort of space in which these relationships can develop. Often they will exist between cultures and institutions, representing zones whereby people from different backgrounds can come together to participate on an equal footing. By existing outside institutional structures, and avoiding the limiting requirements of being within a bureaucracy, trading zones present an opportunity for people to work together and create solutions for problems that couldn't even be conceived of or articulated in more traditional silo mentalities. Trading zones start with an assumption of difference, and intertwine process with product to create shared benefits and outcomes that can be spread widely. It should not be hard to see that these ideas can be applied to helping to overcome disablism, where difference needs to be understood and appropriate support provided, so that everyone can participate equally. For disabled people trading zones are a way of being fully engaged in the processes of change that affect them. For other actors they offer a more successful route to coordinating and developing challenges to disablism.

The characteristics of effective trading zones are discussed below.

They increase adaptive potential

If messy problems don't have clear solutions, how will we know whether trading zones are effective? The focus will be less on particular issues, although effectiveness in these terms is still important, and more on the quality of interaction between people, and the effectiveness of trading zones needs to be understood in these terms. The originating issue of the trading zone may develop and change over time and as such it is the capacity to adapt to future change that matters. A successful trading zone is one that:

○   makes progress in tackling issues identified through a
    process of 'growing up together'
○   has created new relationships that provide ongoing
    capacity for future problem solving
○   or both of the above.

They work towards a shared goal

That's not to say that trading zones do not need to have a clear aim – indeed a shared goal is critical. The point is that the goal shouldn't be too closely defined from the outset as new possibilities could be thwarted through being over-prescriptive. The trading zone should aim to create something new; problems are created if the goal is just to report back to a government minister who will then get all the credit for implementing the ideas of the people in the trading zone. It should avoid the pitfalls of setting up a 'task force' or the like.

They ensure equal communication

A great deal of effort must be put into ensuring that relationships in the trading zone are equal and that communication can occur without particular groups feeling alienated. It means preparing people in advance, helping them to understand something about the people they're about to work with and developing a shared language for communicating with one another. It will mean developing ways of including people who do not use speech for communication or who could be isolated and confined in their own homes to ensure equality of participation. Independent advocacy will be vital.[20] It will often require people who are 'interactional experts': people who can work the trading floor, brokering deals, translating and helping to create codes that enable fair exchange to take place. The skill is in preventing the trading zone turning into a fight because of frustration. Indeed, a demilitarised zone is a prerequisite to an effective trading zone.

They use difference positively

Effective trading zones require an understanding on the part of all the participants that it is a good thing to bring different people together. It's not about creating tidy groups of people who will have the same opinion. As Galison says of trading zones in science, 'It is the disorder of the scientific community – the laminated, finite, partially independent strata supporting one another; it is the disunification of science – the intercalation of different patterns of argument – that is responsible for its strength and coherence.'[21]

The trading zone certainly shouldn't deny the culture of any of the groups or individuals coming into it. It should look for the elements that can contribute to the task at hand, always focusing on what you can do not what you can't do. It's not a way of getting everybody to think and be the same. 'The many traditions coordinate with one another without homogenisation. Different traditions…meet – even transform one another – but for all that do not lose their separate identities and practices.'[22]

Or another way of putting it might be to compare the trading zone to a jazz band: 'All the members have expertise in their own field, but they have to be able to relate to one another and the context they're in…they need to be able to pick up from one another and develop the work further. The sum is greater than the parts and the whole process is generative rather than passive.'[23]

They are open to view

The most effective trading zones are open; the default setting is honesty and open communication. While there may be practical constraints on the number of relationships that can be sustained, other people should be able to look in and offer new ideas. It shouldn't be a club.

They encourage and facilitate informality

Good trading zones are likely to have an informal element. As Susan Scott-Parker says, 'Small talk can lead to big talk' – friendship can be the most important lubricant to trade there is. This means creating the conditions for participants getting to know things about people that aren't to do with the primary reason for their being in the trading zone.

They are temporary

There will be a continuous process of creating and reconfiguring relationships in trading zones. Some will work, others won't. But if the above characteristics are in place, a trading zone has a lot better chance of success. It certainly shouldn't become an institution in its own right. While there may be light structures put in place to support and facilitate the trading zone, they will disappear; however, trading zones may create new institutions and structures.

They promote a creative environment

Most importantly, trading zones work if they have the buzz and energy that comes from people thinking laterally and being open to working with new ideas. Of course it's impossible to just clap your hands and make a meeting 'creative' but the above characteristics will go some way to help.

The aim shouldn't be to create 'disability trading zones', which only include the current actors in debates about disability, but instead to create new trading zones on areas that have relevance to disabled people but also to other people. Disabled people should help to initiate and certainly be part of these trading zones. So, there might be a trading zone for better design, or to help develop best practice for flexible working practices or to develop new methods of influencing public behaviour. These are all ideas we'll return to later in the report.

It can be very threatening to expose your ideas and working methods to people who might be seen as 'the enemy'. The incentives for getting people involved in trading zones, for getting them to work outside their existing institution, also need to be addressed. People inside an organisation can often find it very difficult to see what they might get out of meeting other people from very different cultures. The status quo can feel comfortable and it can be difficult to see what people outside could possibly contribute. We'll return to some methods for overcoming this later in the report.

The three chapters that follow each cover a theme that was seen by disabled people and experts that we spoke to as areas where change was most urgent, not just for disabled people but for everyone. We'll return to some specific ideas for how new trading zones could be established in the final chapter of the report. But first, let's get to work.

3. Work revisited

Towards flexible work and personalised support

'I would love to have a job, but I know it is hard,' Toby Hewson explains. 'I went for an interview and I got it, but after ten weeks they kicked me out.' Toby's optimism and excitement about his new job was dispelled when his employer refused to buy some equipment that would enable him to do his job properly. He knew that what they'd done was illegal under the Disability Discrimination Act but, as he said, 'I haven't got time to start fighting.'

Work is an integral part of our individual and collective identity. It brings perceptions of worth to us as individuals and, at a societal level, higher productivity and employment levels are key indicators of success. So it matters that disabled people find themselves disadvantaged in accessing work. And it's not that disabled people aren't interested in working: Toby is one of the third of disabled people – the 'missing million'[24] – who are out of work but would like a job. So we can quickly dismiss any suggestion that the issue lies with a mass unwillingness to work on the part of disabled people. The economy is losing out on these people's talents and abilities and efforts to get disabled people into work are vital if equality for disabled people is to be achieved.

The DDA requires employers to make 'reasonable adjustments' to enable equal access to work for disabled people, and the government has attempted to help people in the process of finding work through the New Deal for Disabled People and the system of Jobcentre Plus

and jobcentres, which provide disability employment advisors (DEAs). But something isn't working.

Many more disabled people who want to work would be able to work with changes in employment practices and a proactive – but not expensive – approach to adaptations within the workplace. However, although this would move things on a great deal, we are arguing that a more radical approach is needed so that many more disabled people are fully included in the workplace, and their talent unleashed.

One reason for exclusion is the systemic barriers to getting into work if you are a disabled person. Gaining the qualifications to meet a job's requirements, for example, means overcoming more obstacles than a non-disabled person has to in the current system, as does using the transport system to get to a job interview. But there is also the question of what the workplace, using the term in its broadest sense, is like. This is the focus of this chapter and it's here we can learn something from the women's movement. It is 30 years since the Sex Discrimination Act was passed, and yet women still complain of a workplace that is designed for men, and a very particular model of working. So while the legislative requirements and policy shifts may have helped a little, they have only had an impact at the margins of the workplace. The fundamental structures and cultures remain embedded – leaving those who don't fit them, for whatever reason, excluded and what they can contribute untapped.

This chapter proposes that part of the problem is that 'work' and 'welfare' are currently treated as static, separate and rigid concepts and this is to the detriment of everyone, not just disabled people. But if we take as our starting point the idea of a flexible system of work and a personalised system of support, which complement one another, we can develop more humane approaches to economic and social life.

Work in flux

Our experience of work is changing. For more and more people the good old days of 9 to 5 are over; we are increasingly facing the always-on, access-all-areas workplace. Unsurprisingly, this shift has its downsides. Growing numbers of us are complaining of high stress,

increasing isolation and less time to do the things we want to do.[25] 'Work–life balance' is rising fast up the agenda, not least for those cabinet ministers who really do seem to have resigned to spend more time with their families. And in a recent survey by the Department of Trade and Industry, 93 per cent of people said they would like to have more flexible working arrangements.

By the end of the twentieth century an hour's work was on average 25 times more productive than at the beginning of the century[26] and it's tempting to apply the same techniques and mindsets to deliver still more. The relentless competitive drive of a globalised economy encourages this pursuit of short-term gain further. So it's still the workaholics who are getting promoted, and not trailblazers of the flexible working that we all profess to want. But the temptations of an economy where working harder and longer has delivered productivity rewards in the past are actually holding us back.

Questions are beginning to be asked about whether the macho 'work hard, play hard' culture is as valuable for productivity and the bottom line as some people might think. As we will see in the next chapter, our economy is increasingly fuelled by ideas and a premium placed on creativity and innovation rather than the hours we work. In this context, tired and stressed modern workers aren't just unhappy – they are suboptimal. A Finnish report about the future of work found that: 'more than a half of the Finns are suffering from some degree of symptoms of burnout…one in five was very tired in their work. The latest studies show that there were more exhausted workers among the under-30s than among 50-year-olds.'[27]

Creativity cannot possibly flourish under such conditions, particularly when the innovators of the future are burning out before they even get going. What organisations need is greater flexibility. Many of the things that would make paid work possible for and appealing to disabled people are precisely the things that bodies like the Work-Life Balance campaign have been pushing for many years: better rewards and more facility for part-time working, more provision for working from home and greater flexibility in when required hours are worked, for example.

If such measures were incorporated into workplace culture, not just (barely) tolerated by employers, disabled people who might be unable to work a full day in an office, or who currently find transport to work impossible, would be able to apply for and hold down paid work confidently. And the benefits would be felt by all of us; for example, parents would be able to take their children to school and work at home when a child was ill without worrying about job security. As with product and service design, which we will look at in the next chapter, putting disabled people at the heart of designing the more flexible workplace would deliver clear benefits to us all. Among other things, we need role models to show us the value of this creative model – Scope's Diversity Works programme (see box) aims to do just this. We also need the benefits of the 'business case for flexible working' to be made real. Disabled people have an incentive to do both of these things as a more flexible workplace is fundamental to enabling them to undertake the paid work from which they are currently excluded.

Diversity works

Scope's Diversity Works programme is going about getting more disabled people into work in three ways:

O   by creating a network of work opportunities to which disabled people can be appointed, and then enabled to move onwards to senior posts, across a wide range of organisations

O   by supporting disabled people with underdeveloped potential to obtain work and continually develop their work and management skills through online training and mentoring and practical work experience

O   by making changes to the work environment through disability equality training of employers including managers and staff, changes to human resources and recruitment policies, and an exemplary approach to addressing practical barriers.

Andy Rickell, who heads the programme, describes the vicious circle that led Scope to set it up:

The need for Diversity Works arises because of the failure of work environments to address institutional disablism, which in turn has denied disabled people the opportunities to acquire the work experience to skill them for senior posts, which in turn means the culture of work environments has not been influenced by disabled people operating at senior levels within organisations, hence perpetuating institutional disablism.

But revolutionising the workplace is not just about increasing flexibility within the current model of paid work, it's about creating a new model which values and accords status to contributions of all kinds. For example work with young disabled people has shown that they are not so much concerned with contributing through paid work as contributing positively to the lives of people around them – such as being a good friend, brother or sister or valuable part of their immediate community.[28] Volunteer work remains unrecognised despite a large increase in participants across all demographics, and carers are still undervalued, despite their incredible contributions. Developing a more flexible definition of work incorporating these and many other important activities doesn't replace the argument that everyone should have an equal opportunity to work; it enriches it.

Workfare and welfare

Unfortunately, the meaning of work within policy frameworks has not caught up with the massive change in its meaning in society at large. Work is assumed to be full-time, office-based and paid. It is separate from the rest of our lives, so that work and life need to be balanced and juggled as if they were discrete activities. Perhaps this wouldn't be important were it not for the fact that access to support systems, both financial and social, are determined by whether an individual falls within the parameters of this increasingly outdated notion of work. We can see this in the government's manifesto

commitment: 'for people unable to take up paid work, we are committed to offer security' or as one minister put it: 'Work for those who can, support for those who cannot'.[29]

The implication of this is that those who are not working are either failing to fulfil their role as a citizen or else in need of support. Through making this the starting point of government policy a profound series of unintended consequences have served to stagnate discussions around disabled people and work. In order to determine whether someone out of work is worthy of support, the benefits system is configured to create a clear blue divide between those who are able to work and those who are not. This is policy more suited to a previous era where jobs were for life and flexibility meant 'any colour you like, as long as it's black' and it certainly seems incompatible with the kinds of flexible workplace described above. It is also incompatible with the fact that people's impairments are not static: they may change over time, even over the course of a week or a month. Its implication is either you're in or you're out.

And once you're out, you're definitely out. Dean, whose story as a disabled parent we heard about in the first chapter, lives in Nottingham and, having done a few paid jobs over the years, he now works mainly in voluntary organisations: 'I would get a "proper job" but it's not financially viable. Every time I change jobs it affects everything else. Far more disabled people would work if it didn't take months to get back your benefits.' The drawn-out process of assessing whether you fit the 'disabled' label makes it far harder for people to move in and out of work when they can. As Dean says, 'my livelihood shouldn't be decided on whether I can make a cup of tea or not.' The system is not configured to be responsive to people whose situations may change from week-to-week or even day-to-day.

All of this indicates that we need to ask whether we can really bring about change for the better by making workfare our starting point. It seems to fail disabled people, and ultimately it will let everyone down by denying the complex relationship between work and the rest of our lives. It's not so much that we need to *balance* work and life; more, we need to find ways of *integrating* them.

By thinking in these terms, the starting point is less about labelling individuals and placing them within fixed parameters of work or support; instead, we should focus on providing support according to need. These needs might be the result of an impairment, a bereavement or a birth. Perhaps it's time to move away from fixed labels and accept that as we all move through our life cycles our support needs will vary. All any of us want is a level of support that matches our need. For this to happen, though, the system of support would need to be personalised.

Things are getting personal

Think back to Toby whose story begins this chapter. In order even to get into the job he needed a good education, technical equipment to reduce the disability he experienced, excellent 24-hour personal support assistant services, and appropriate housing and transport. The issue wasn't getting into work per se, but the ways in which life and work were integrated. The challenge for policy-makers is to develop an approach to support that puts the user at the centre, so that users are empowered to shape the services they access to meet their needs, and integrate this with a form of work that makes the most of each person's potential. In order to address this challenge we can no longer think about disability and work in a vacuum. We need to consider the public services that provide support to disabled people and reforming them to put the person at their centre.

How might this reform be brought about? Charles Leadbeater has recently argued that the first step comes from seeing public services as scripts with the script determining the parts played by the actors involved.[30] So if, for example, we consider the script of having a meal at a restaurant, it would run something like this: arrive at restaurant and be shown to table; examine menu; place order with waiter; food delivered to table; eat; ask for the bill; pay; leave. Fast-food and self-service restaurants are both examples of service innovation through the way they rewrote the script. In self-service restaurants, for example, the 'users' take on some of the role of the waiters through helping themselves.

So really the question we must ask is how can we rewrite the script of support services so that they are more responsive to their users? Direct Payments are a very particular example of an attempt by government to put the user in the driving seat. Underlying this policy is the view that users will know better than producers what services and support they need, and therefore they are better placed to allocate the resources. Direct Payments set disabled people free as consumers, giving them the funds to buy the services they need. A market of service providers is created, with the producers of the services needing to respond to the demands of the consumers. The role played by the state is rewritten: they are no longer allocating the resources; instead they are providing information about the choices on offer, and ensuring a high-quality supply of the services.

Turning users into consumers does seem to be a way of placing their concerns at the heart of service provision, but the problem is that it places a high level of responsibility and expectation on those users. In order to make fully informed decisions users need to be able to digest and interpret information that is often so complex that even the professionals and policy wonks struggle to make sense of it. They need to act as individual integrators of a range of services that cut across the traditional silos of housing, transport and education. And in a system where supply of good services is not unlimited, anyone without sharp elbows and a mind for numbers risks losing out. People don't – and can't – always shop around for a good service or the best deal. A personalised system is about far more than simply handing over a pile of money.

A system that is personalised offers a meaningful way of connecting the individual to their society by enabling users to have a more direct input into the script by which their services are written and delivered. Disabled people, rather than being treated as pathetic objects of pity and in need of care, become conscious actors. The services disabled people access in a personalised system are ones that have been shaped to meet their needs – because of their active participation in the shaping and design of the script in the first place.

So what might a personalised system look like? First, returning to

Dean's words, 'service providers have got to see the person and ask them what do they need to live their lives?' The starting point of a personalised system is a question about what an individual needs in the broadest sense of the word. A person's impairment means they will require some sort of support, but they may also have aspirations and wants that can only be uncovered through an extended dialogue. For Dean, getting people to understand that he might have goals and dreams is a major challenge: 'Because I have a speech impairment people tend not to listen. They can't believe I have something valid to say.' It is only through uncovering these broader needs, rather than simply a person's support needs, that the foundations can be laid for a personalised system.

Secondly, a personalised system would have many 'simplicity brokers' or 'advocates'. These are people who work with the users to help them unlock these needs and aspirations. They would also provide the map by which users can navigate complex public services. In Dean's view, 'services are geared up for single issues and create their own little kingdoms. What you end up with is a complete nightmare for people trying to access services. You've either got to know the system very well or you fall by the wayside. You can go for years without getting what you want.' The job of the simplicity brokers would be to understand and work with users, while understanding the full range of choices and pathways that could be taken through the system.

Thirdly, in order to do their job properly these simplicity brokers would need to work closely with other professionals. We can see from the example of the In Control programme (see box) that it would only be possible to assemble solutions personalised to individual need if services work in partnership. The simplicity brokers would be the gateway to a flexible network of partnerships that developed according to the changing circumstances of the user. In this way users are not simply choosing between a range of pre-organised packages, but actually determining the very shape of their package in the first place.

Fourthly, users would still retain ultimate control over the services they received through retaining their spending power. In this way users never become dependent on the judgements of professionals – they retain their position of being free to challenge advice.

Don't you just love being 'in control'?

'We're trying to turn around the relationship between the state and the person', Simon Duffy tells us calmly. He's coordinator of the In Control programme, which has been developed – by the Department of Health's Valuing Support team, Mencap, Helen Sanderson Associates, Northwest Training and Development Team and Paradigm – to help people with learning difficulties shape the kind of support they access. The programme began in autumn 2003 and is working across six local authorities to develop a template for what they're calling self-directed support (SDS; www.selfdirectedsupport.org). As Simon tells us, 'We place the onus on the person, not the care system.' Self-directed support has seven stages for the person in question:

○ *assessment* – finding out what support you are entitled to
○ *supported decisions* – working out what help you might need with any decision-making
○ *person-centred planning* – working out what you want to do and what help you will need to achieve it
○ *support planning* – agreeing what you are going to do with the local authority
○ *individualised funding* – managing the money for your support in the way that suits you best
○ *implementation* – organising and managing your support and making sure you work within the rules
○ *review* – learning about what is working and not working and changing it when necessary.[31]

In Control is also taking an innovative approach to spreading the idea of SDS. As Simon says, 'There's a lot of "do this" and "don't do this" in this field and not a lot of explanation about how it can be

> done. But we think if we create a system that works, we should publish it and then let people take it and adapt it to their own circumstances – along the same lines as open source computer software.' The In Control team hopes that the idea will eventually spread to benefit not just people with learning difficulties but people across the board who need support to live the lives they want to lead.

It would be too easy to dismiss the idea of a personalised system as impossible to deliver and pay for on such a large scale. But by considering the costs of a personalised support system longitudinally and holistically the wider social and economic benefits it would bring are clear. In fact, it is only through personalising support that everyone will truly be able to achieve their full potential. Harnessing the productivity and creativity of the thousands of disabled people unable to work currently can only be a good thing. Furthermore, there are social benefits to creating a personalised system whereby users participate in the design of their support and services. As Charles Leadbeater has recently argued, 'involved users are likely to be more committed to a successful outcome'. Spending less money on support services that don't help individuals should never be seen as a better investment of public money.

So, in a personalised system, many of the current dichotomies are removed. Support is something that is recognised as being of universal importance, and something that no doubt everyone will need to access at some point in their life. The kind of provision on offer is related more precisely to need, rather than to whether a person is deemed 'incapacitated' or not. Work in this context becomes the contribution any individual is able to make to society rather than only meaningful if performed full-time, in a traditional work environment. In a personalised system, the opposite of being disabled is not being able-bodied, it's being enabled.

Disablism throws debates about work–life balance into sharp relief. Disabled individuals must have an equal right to work. But for that to happen the starting point for meaningful change should be to provide personalised systems rather than 'workfare' – systems that seek to integrate more flexible types of work and support. We need to lose the restrictive definitions of 'work' and 'incapacity' and begin by considering the needs and aspirations of individuals.

4. The engine of difference

Disability, innovation and creativity

'It's really very simple,' Jeremy Myerson tells us as we sit in a meeting room at the Royal College of Art (RCA) in London. He draws two circles – one inside the other – in his notebook. 'Instead of designing products for this tiny group of people who are "average",' he points to the smaller circle in the middle, 'you design them for everyone.' He moves his pen out and taps it on the far larger circle.

It does sound simple when you put it like that but how do you go about practising 'inclusive design'? Myerson is co-director of the Helen Hamlyn Research Centre at the RCA, which has been learning and teaching others how to do it since 1991. 'You need to interact with people who are different – older people or disabled people, for example, thinking of them as the potential user rather than a young Mr or Mrs Average.'

But this means going against almost 50 years of practice in the design and marketing worlds. It started in the 1950s and 1960s with industrial designers like Henry Dreyfuss whose team developed 'Joe' and 'Josephine', typical American models that could be used in the design of everything from airline seating to power tools. The way they created Joe and Josephine was to make thousands of measurements of Americans and then simply come up with an average figure for everything from size to reach, strength to agility. At the time this was a great leap forward – actually designing objects around people was a novelty, with most machines designed by engineers more interested in what was easy to make rather than what was easy to use. But the process of designing for the middle, the average person, has driven mass marketing and mass consumerism ever since.

This isn't good for anyone, least of all for disabled people. A recent survey showed that nine out of ten people over the age of 50 had trouble opening food packaging in the last year. An incredible 71 per cent of those people sustained an injury from these badly designed products.[32] We perhaps shouldn't find this at all surprising – at the moment new products are not even tested on Joe and Josephine average. Focus groups are often made up of people who want the cash – young, strong people with good coordination and excellent eyesight.

This chapter provides the rationale for engagement between designers of products and services and disabled people in the design process. Myerson and his colleagues have a body of evidence which shows inclusive design to be better for disabled people, as well as for everyone else. This is valuable in itself; but what should become clear throughout the chapter is that a society with more and better innovators will not only improve the quality of individual products and services, but has the ability to improve its overall 'adaptive potential' – its ability to survive in a changing environment.

Ever increasing circles

We can look at the value of inclusive design in a series of three expanding circles. Unlike the circles above, at the centre of this set are disabled people who undoubtedly benefit from user-centred design.

There are myriad examples of this: the ''ello' mobile phone, winner of the Design Business Association Design Challenge 2003 is ready to use when opened, and the keypad automatically rises to make the buttons easy to use. This is particularly important to disabled people for whom a mobile phone can be central to staying independent. Ricability, a national research charity dedicated to providing independent information to disabled and older consumers, has a whole catalogue of products for 'easier and safer living'. These include alternative switches that work for most kinds of appliances, are larger than the standard version and are activated with only light pressure. 'Talking Labels' also feature – a handheld reader uses barcodes to identify foods, clothes and CDs among other things. They also highlight innovations as simple as adjustable height work surfaces, sinks and hobs.

Moving out, there is a broader circle including groups like mothers with small children who will benefit if disabled people are put at the centre of the design process. Take the example of the introduction of new buses in London to make them easier to access by wheelchair users. Of course, accessibility for wheelchair users was improved, but in the first few months the number of mothers and children also using the service increased rapidly.[33] Then there's the housing association in Coventry that made its information more accessible for partially sighted and blind people in 2003. What they found was that by recording housing information onto audio tapes they were serving people from ethnic minorities better as well – many of those for whom English was a second language could understand the spoken word, but couldn't read it.[34] Those nine out of ten people having trouble with food packaging are also better off at Waitrose since Goodwin and Hartshorn's Opening Up project produced inclusively designed tins, jars and plastic packets.[35] Everyone else is better off, too, as the estimated cost to the NHS and the tax payer of those injured by badly designed packaging is roughly £11 million per year.[36]

Finally everyone else, including Joe and Josephine average, are advantaged in a world where signs are clearer, buildings are more accessible and telephones are easier to use. One example of this is the 'big button phone' of British Telecom (BT). The design was the result of collaboration between BT and the Sensory Design Services, an inclusive design consultancy affiliated to the Royal National Institute for the Blind. It aimed to create a phone that partially sighted people or those with coordination problems would find easy to use. One month after its launch it became the fourth best-selling phone in BT's range and the ninth best seller on the high street.[37]

So it's clear that inclusive design can produce better products and services not just for disabled people, but for everyone else into the bargain. The commercial imperative to roll out inclusive design is there and it will only increase as society ages: in 2003, 10 per cent of 16 to 24-year-olds were disabled and this proportion increased to one-third in the 50 to retirement age category. The imperative may well be compounded if, as Julia Huber and Paul Skidmore suggest, baby boomers don't just swell the size of the older population, but increase its political voice and make it more demanding.[38]

Inclusive design needs the involvement of disabled people to create a stronger model of user design. Business thinker Gary Hamel says simply that successful innovation 'must begin by developing an experiential sense of what it means to be a customer'.[39] Disabled people represented a market of 8.6 million customers at the last count and their experiences aren't yet feeding through into processes of innovation. But the role of disabled people as innovators can and should be more active; we should include disabled people in the design process because they are good at it. There are two main reasons for this.

First, disabled people are often outstanding problem solvers because they have to be. It became clear in the previous chapter on work that life for disabled people at the moment is a series of challenges to be overcome; Rachel Hurst summed it up when she told us 'to do anything, I have to solve six different problems'. Making the workplace more accessible is not sufficient if negotiating the transport system to get to work isn't possible: what good is a ramp at the entrance to a restaurant if you can't get out of bed in the morning? The big message here is obviously that piecemeal solutions to access problems are not sufficient. It also tells us that, having struggled with a world that is only sporadically accessible, disabled people have developed a wealth of experience as serial innovators.

Secondly, innovative ideas are more likely to come from those who have a new or different angle on old problems. As Sandra Yates, chairman of Saatchi and Saatchi Australia puts it, 'good ideas can come from anyone, anywhere, but they are least likely to come from those who have been socialised into conventional business behavior'.[40] Hamel echoes this; he says that it is 'on the fringe…of technology, entertainment, fashion and politics…where new possibilities present themselves'.[41] Disabled people clearly fit the bill. Today, ideas are central to a flourishing economy. The rise of the internet and the proliferation and transparency of information means that 'knowledge' alone is no longer enough. As Jack Welch has said, 'the winners in the new economy will be…those who have captured the best and brightest ideas people'. Some of these will be the disabled people currently excluded from the workplace.

Interestingly, these 'advantages' should disappear as disabled people begin to enjoy greater equality. But greater participation of disabled people in innovation in the short term may just be the necessary trigger for creating an altogether different, and better, system of innovation for everyone in the future.

The innovation imperative

But why does innovation matter? Back to those two types of problem that Jake Chapman identifies, 'difficulties' and 'messes', that we introduced in chapter 2.[42] A difficulty is a problem where the tools for solving it are well understood. That's not to say that it won't take a great deal of time and expertise to solve the problem, but it is agreed that the problem is eventually soluble through expert judgement and hard work. When it comes to messes, there is certainly no agreement about how to go about solving the problem, indeed there is often no real agreement about what the problem is.

When we look around us, at the challenges facing us globally – environmentally, economically and not least in achieving equality for currently excluded groups – we see a lot of messes. While some progress has been made solving some of them, the overall challenge can seem overwhelming when we look at the rate of progress in developing solutions. In short we're finding and creating messes faster than we know how to solve them. Thomas Homer Dixon calls this the 'ingenuity gap'.[43]

Nature, perhaps the most resilient system we know of, reacts to messes by innovating. It creates 'variety', a whole host of different solutions. It does this constantly, increasing its 'adaptive potential' by distributing this ability. No matter what the centre says, specific environments and contexts will require new ways of doing things of their own. In human systems, innovation – the ability to create and turn new ideas to products, services, business processes and organisational structures – is the key to providing the greatest possible variety of solutions. A certain amount of trial and error is necessary in untangling messes; they can't be objectively analysed and fixed so solutions must be judged by their outcomes. If we accept this, then it becomes clear that maximising the size and diversity of our pool of innovators gives us the best possible chance of starting to untangle the many important messes we face. Any group that is currently excluded from the process of innovation could have something to offer, but including disabled people, who are proven innovators, is likely to be even more effective.

The second part of effective untangling is about how to harness the lessons learnt from that pool of solutions – innovation independent of strong feedback mechanisms is meaningless as we take nothing from it. A one-off conversation is not enough if no one knows quite what the outcome of a 'solution' might be. What is needed is a learning system, where developing solutions is an iterative and continuous process.

Upstream engagement

It is important to remember that stakeholders must be 'upstream' of the innovation process from inception to implementation. In the industrial era innovation was something done behind closed doors by expert 'innovators' in research labs away from prying eyes. All you did was hire bright people, got them to innovate and then patented their inventions before selling them to the public 'downstream'. This process is beginning to change and is increasingly seen as ineffective by the world's most innovative companies and business experts. People like Henry Chesbrough advocate a process of 'open innovation' where the innovation process is more networked to the outside world.[44] Gary Hamel, too, says that the challenge for systemic innovation is to 'create a process where new ideas can be validated by peers – not by the hierarchy'.[45] The evidence of how this can work practically in the field of disability is beginning to emerge.

In the field of design, take Natascha Frensch's 'Read Regular', a typeface she developed while at the Helen Hamlyn Centre, which is easier for dyslexic people, and everyone else, to read. In developing her design she tested her new typeface against conventional ones with nearly 100 dyslexic people, children and adults, constantly amending and improving it. The process was an ongoing conversation, where participants saw their feedback translated into changes made to the design.

What we're learning is that for these conversations to work everyone needs to speak the same language. Bengt-Åke Lundvall, an economist, talks of innovation taking place when there is a 'collision' between technical opportunity and user needs.[46] But for that collision to be productive, not destructive, shared 'channels and codes' of information, built on mutual trust and effective communication, have to exist. These lessons have yet to be fully explored and are far from being applied widely.

The message is clear. Disabled people are often excellent innovators and have lots of ideas. In the short term the involvement of disabled people in design processes can help to deliver better products and services for everyone: an easy-to-read plaque on a postbox, a big button phone or a shower with a better dial. In the long run, asking disabled people to be at the heart of the design process could help to revolutionise our whole system of public services and of business. Disabled people can teach us to listen to users first, second and last so that the people who matter create solutions, tell us what really works, and everyone reaps the benefits.

Innovation that places disabled people at the heart of a process that will improve everyone's quality of life also does something more: it starts to get rid of the 'them and us' distinction, which is at the root of the discrimination still faced by disabled people. This happens at both ends of the design process: 'upstream inclusion' of disabled people from the outset reflects and builds an appreciation of their contribution; and the ability of everyone to use the final product or service allows disabled people to be part of the 'mainstream'.

5. The empty plinth

Influencing public attitudes and behaviour towards disabled people

…having this statue helps to articulate a reality – we exist, we're part of the fabric of society and that being 'different' because of an impairment or having the experience of 'disability', doesn't merit being ignored, hidden away or made to feel ashamed.

comment on the BBC's *Ouch!* message board

TRAVULGAR SQUARE

headline in the *Sun*, March 2004

When it was announced that Marc Quinn's statue of Alison Lapper was one of the two winners of the competition to fill the fourth plinth in London's Trafalgar Square, controversy ensued. When the statue is unveiled in 2005 it will be a 15ft high white marble sculpture of Alison when she was eight and a half months pregnant. Alison was born with short limbs. The flurry of media activity brought home how far away we are from a society where attitudes mean that disabled people are talked about in terms of their merits as people rather than looking at their impairment first. In the initial batch of newspaper coverage, little was made of Alison's credentials as an artist, for instance.

Ask someone if they discriminate against disabled people and they'll almost certainly say no. But dig a little deeper and it becomes clear that they're not completely sure what they think. As the

Employers' Forum on Disability put it, 'They will usually express considerable goodwill towards a group they tend to regard as unfortunate victims…. They will also tend to display a deep reluctance to accept disabled people on equal terms. This is often based on unquestioned, deeply-held negative assumptions or stereotypes.'[47]

Coupled to this, the attitudes of non-disabled people to disabled people are often irrational. It's not easy from a distance to understand why people think the way they do about disability. Their attitudes can be based on feelings of embarrassment, pity, guilt, being patronising and even revulsion, which are difficult to get to the bottom of. People also have trouble talking to disabled people or even just about disability on a more conceptual level in a way that is now much less the case with discussions about gender or race. They are often scared that they will get the language wrong, look in the wrong place or say something that will offend the person in question.

In short, disablism is rife in our society and often rooted in the attitudes of individual citizens but it's not simple to explain or reason with. The question is how best to eliminate it. The assumption has been that this is something for government to deal with, but formal legislation, such as the DDA, and institutions, such as the DRC, are a necessary but insufficient step towards eradicating discrimination. Just using legislation to achieve equality creates an atmosphere of people being 'told off' for their behaviour. We need to probe deeper to develop forms of intervention that are going to be more effective and legitimate.

The politics of public behaviour

The art of government has been around for a long time. The rule of law has been developed and improved over millennia; economics as a discipline of policy levers and instruments has enjoyed 300 years of intensive development. These provide the basis for the 'carrots and sticks' of policy that governments use regularly and think tanks and lobbyists are prone to call for. But there is a growing recognition, as a forthcoming report from the Prime Minister's Strategy Unit suggests, that these blunt instruments on which government has traditionally relied – taxes and subsidies, regulations and legal sanctions – are not sufficiently sophisticated to engineer the deep shifts in personal responsibility and behaviour that are increasingly being asked of them.[48]

The art of directly influencing public attitudes and behaviour, through 'soft' measures such as advertising and public information, is relatively new. Evidence about which approaches work well, in what situations and why, is patchy, based on half-formed theories and false assumptions that fail to take sufficient account of the nuances of human behaviour. If the law provides the sticks and economic policy adds some carrots, efforts so far to use information and advertising to influence public behaviour could be summed up as being regarded as 'sermons', partly because of where they emanate from.

The underlying problem with many efforts of influencing the public is that they are still reliant on an outdated model of government's relationship with citizens and consumers. The expert-led, command-and-control approach that came to the fore in wartime propaganda, and persisted in public awareness campaigns until the 1970s and 1980s, is no longer adequate for the complex, diverse and individualised society of today.

What it comes down to is that we are no longer sure whether we trust governments to tell us how to think or behave. Deference towards traditional institutional authority in general and political authority, in particular, has plummeted, at the same time as the value attached to personal autonomy has increased. Grounding attempts to influence public behaviour in legitimate sources of expertise is proving more and more difficult for government, too, as the recent controversy over MMR vaccinations showed. And the days when a minister could in all candour state that: 'In the case of nutrition and health, just as in the case of education, the gentleman in Whitehall really does know better what is good for people than people know themselves'[49] are certainly now long gone.

But what has changed to make this the case? Social changes over the past 30 years have cast doubt on the idea of public opinion as homogenous and readily identified. People are now acknowledged to exhibit a far greater diversity of individual motivations, beliefs and behaviours. Tom Bentley sums up this trend: 'As societies have become more diverse, more complex and more open, the range of issues and social groupings has become far harder to corral into coherent policy platforms or voter coalitions.'[50]

The media is also changing. Traditional mass channels such as newspapers and television are diversifying and facing competition from new media and peer-to-peer networks. New forms of communication such as email and mobile phones make it easier to maintain extended networks of acquaintances, which often become the anchors of identity and behaviour. This encourages a trend whereby porous social networks (instead of membership of large social groups) become the primary arbiters of behaviour. As Andrew Curry argues: 'People's trust is migrating towards "my world group" and away from sources of authority. So what we will end up with is people in those "my world groups" acting as gatekeepers, where trust is formed around word of mouth.'[51]

These trends do not sit well with conventional notions of public opinion and behaviour, capable of being shaped and manipulated through the mass media by centralised governments. A more diverse public makes the mobilisation of public opinion more difficult, but it also makes the use of softer influencing techniques more essential, as traditional policy tools struggle to adapt to the complexities of modern society.

This matters for the argument of this report because developing more sophisticated and successful methods of influencing public attitudes and behaviour towards disabled people is a pressing concern to achieving a better society for everyone. Among the disabled people we spoke to there was a recognition that the tools developed so far cannot provide the answer to everything. The Disability Discrimination Act, simply as a legal device, is limited in what it can achieve. The Disability Rights Commission (soon to be subsumed into the Commission on Equality and Human Rights) can only help so many people fight inequality individually.

What is needed is something that can make change contagious.

Beyond carrots, sticks and sermons

The viral nature of behaviour change has been well described by Malcolm Gladwell who coined the term 'tipping point' to describe the point at which an idea or practice is transmitted to more than one person at each transaction. He uses it to explain how small, or even imperceptible, alterations in the environment can initiate changes in behaviour. For example, removing the graffiti from the New York subway could be seen as a tipping point in the decline of crime in New York.

We could also look to business. In the 50 years that government has spent trying to figure out how to influence public behaviour, business has become much more sophisticated in how it understands, shapes and adapts to the behaviour of its customers. Shoshana Zuboff and James Maxmin have argued that companies need to focus less on individual transactions and invest more in building 'relationship value' with customers and other firms if they are to thrive.[52] The emerging field of 'social marketing' also has clear lessons here. It places the emphasis on viewing the change being advocated from the potential adopters' perspective.[53]

Such thinking challenges the 'billiard ball' conceptualisation of public opinion and behaviour, whereby citizens respond neatly to a series of interventions, as a ball does to a well-placed cue shot. Rather, the process of influencing becomes much more about managing, cultivating and spreading change through networks. What it comes down to is that although there is a lot that government can do to change people's attitudes to disabled people, they can't do it alone. And although disability charities can do a lot, they too cannot do it alone. Increasingly public behaviour is in the hands of a network of actors, and network solutions to influencing public attitudes and behaviour will be required.

Sociologist Manuel Castells proposes that, 'networked organisations out-compete all other forms of organisation, particularly the vertical, rigid, command-and-control bureaucracies'.[54] Network campaigning has been explored by a number of social movements in the past decade with some dramatic manifestations and results; it could also have lessons for helping to influence public behaviour towards disabled people. Think, for example, of the International Campaign to Ban Landmines or the Jubilee 2000 coalition to eradicate the unpayable debts of developing countries. Disability Awareness in Action is a network, too, comprising 3,500 organisations and individuals in 164 countries, providing information to support campaigning for disability rights.

In essence, network campaigning allows a diverse grouping of organisations and individuals to participate through commitment to a shared purpose, while remaining autonomous individual agents. In this way it is possible to gain additional leverage through the 'multiplier effect' of having a coherent message and through more efficient deployment of resources and effort, while maintaining flexibility and energy, which more bureaucratic forms of coordination tend to squander. Networks are much more suited to adapting to complex environments where attitudes and responses to messages are diverse.

Network campaigns:

○ have a simple shared goal that is easy to articulate
○ are 'structure light', usually having a very small coordinating secretariat if any at all
○ build a coalition of other organisations containing a range of skills and resources
○ make good use of network technology, treating the many-to-many nature of the internet as an opportunity
○ embrace diversity and openness – it doesn't matter who you are (within limits) as long as you can contribute something to achieving the goal
○ use celebrities to reach the parts they can't – getting noticed can help to build new networks
○ use physical space – making sure campaigners meet face-to-face is important for building a sense of network energy and enthusiasm
○ are time limited – urgency is a campaigner's best friend.[55]

There are two ways that network campaigns could be used to influence public attitudes and challenge disablism. First, by making sure that disabled people are engaged in the development of more network-based means of influencing public behaviour across the board on subjects that don't necessarily spring to mind as 'disability' issues. This might involve disabled people creating relationships with global environmental campaigners, for example. The benefits might not be obvious at first glance but if there's a goal that can be shared (even if it is not the primary goal of either group) then collaboration makes sense.

Secondly, other groups should be joining disabled people in developing network-based campaigns on specific elements of achieving equality. If we are to unlock the benefits of a more flexible system of work and support, and the innovative potential that disabled people possess, disablism needs to be removed as a barrier. One key to this will be spotting those little ideas that can change the world.

Little ideas can go a long way

Little ideas can go a long way in a network. Take the example of Jonah Peretti and his personalised trainers. Nike had created a feature on its website allowing shoppers to customise shoes with words or slogans of their choice. Jonah took them up on this and ordered a pair of shoes customised with the word 'sweatshop'. Nike refused to deliver. But the email conversation between Peretti and the Nike customer services department about why the company wouldn't allow his request was stored on Peretti's computer. Peretti forwarded the email conversation to just 12 friends, but within hours thousands of people had seen the message. Within days the message had been posted on popular discussion sites like Slashdot.org and Plastic.com and was seen by tens of thousands of other internet users. Soon, Peretti was getting calls from journalists and TV producers asking him for interviews. NBC's Today programme flew him to New York to appear live in front of millions of viewers. Once the message was out, there was no going back and suddenly a lot more people knew about sweatshops.[56]

If the disability movement is to foster this kind of simple, contagious message about eliminating discrimination towards disabled people, it will need support and involvement from as many different groups and organisations as possible. The challenge will be how to create new relationships between disabled people and other groups. Disability charities and government departments will need to be more responsive to having their resources and networks used by small groups of people working in networks and other groups will need to be willing to join those networks if they are to be effective.

Why would other people want to get involved and reconfigure their relationships to include disabled people? Well, as we've articulated in the two previous chapters, we believe that there is a long-term interest for everyone in eliminating the discriminatory and negative attitudes towards disabled people that prevent them from playing as valuable a part in society as they could. But while that incentive remains little understood and outside the mainstream, it is here that the government and other large players can lend a hand using their existing financial muscle to influence new relationships.

After a great deal of pressure from them, the Department for Work and Pensions is now getting disabled people into the images used in all government advertising. You might not have noticed, indeed that's part of the point. But the hidden benefit has been in engaging the advertising agencies who create campaigns for everything from targeting benefit fraud to 'doing your bit' for the environment in issues about how disabled people are portrayed. Rather than just focusing on broadcast and billboard advertising they could go further to help reconfigure relationships in a trading zone, to create more network-based approaches to influencing public attitudes and behaviour led by disabled people themselves. This is an idea we will return to in the next chapter.

6. After the party
The next phase of change

This autumn there's going to be a party. All those who've been campaigning and working towards the Disability Discrimination Act and the establishment of a Disability Rights Commission will raise a glass as the final parts of the legislation come into force. There will, of course, be gaps and omissions to be filled and faults in the legislation to be corrected. Plus there is the small matter of how the DRC will manage to keep the flag flying for disabled people as it is subsumed into the new Commission for Equality and Human Rights. But overall there will be a sense that the current chapter of campaigning and legislating is coming to an end and that deserves a celebration. But a question looms – what next?

This report has argued that there is a crying need for further change. The lived experience of disabled people in the UK is still one of far lower opportunity, and access to rights, than for their non-disabled fellow citizens. A lot done, a lot still to do, you might say. What's more, the slow pace of change means that society more widely is missing out on the participation of disabled people, which could lead to improvements in products and services for all of us. So the question is, how can we better understand the challenge of disablism and what strategies for change should be used to overcome it? In this report we have set out an agenda for change that seeks to move beyond the traditional 'carrots, sticks and sermons' approach, which sees legislation and top-down initiatives as the best means of achieving goals.

Change for the better relies on understanding the problem from the perspective of individuals. It is the experiences of those individuals that must be the starting point for any agenda of change. In chapter 3 we took the example of work to underline this argument and asked how to develop an economy that provides work which is flexible enough to make the most of the skills of everybody in our society. Economic success won't be generated through making people work longer hours in more rigid hierarchies subservient to increasingly blinkered profit-making or 'productivity' goals. Increasingly the organisations that attract the best talent and develop the levels of innovation necessary to thrive in the modern world are those that adapt to the needs of their employees. In this more flexible world of work a sensible system of support is needed that provides the kind of personalised services people can access as and when they need to. Disabled people have a stronger interest than most in helping to develop systems of work and support that can achieve this. Employers and the government would do well to help them lead the way to a system that is better for all of us.

If change for the better needs to begin with the experiences and expectations of individuals, then these individuals must be involved in the early shaping and design of products and services. Change will not come from consultation alone. Participation needs to be much deeper than this. Chapter 4 highlighted the ingenuity gap that now faces us. The government rightly puts a strong emphasis on innovation and no self-respecting company would claim not to be innovative and hope to survive. Our products are badly designed in the face of demographic change. We're becoming an older society. By extending the analysis of the inclusive design movement to include products, systems and services that might never see the pencil of a professional designer, we have a template for upstream engagement of people who aren't Joe or Josephine Average. Again, given the opportunity, disabled people could lead the way.

Finally, change will only really come about if attitudes, as well as services and products, begin to shift. Disablism – the discriminatory attitudes and behaviour of individual citizens towards disabled people – is costing us dearly. It holds back millions of disabled people from living the lives they want to lead and contributing to society and the economy in a way that will benefit us all. Carrots and sticks can only take us so far, especially in an era when we're beginning to realise that the state is limited in what it can achieve alone. Change is dependent on the willing participation of a network of actors. We are short of ways to influence public behaviour that avoid indoctrination or sermonising – neither of these is beneficial in the long run. These methods will be more in tune with the network logic of our modern society, working to find contagious ideas that will lead to tipping points being exceeded and change happening.

The political process of the twentieth century has created a framework of legislation that aims to integrate equality into the dignity of the person through human rights and cross-government responsibilities. But government is struggling to adapt and engage with the changing reality of twenty-first century society. Having achieved formal recognition, one challenge for the politics of disability is to avoid disappearance into the fog of implementation, overcome by higher profile equality issues and institutional pecking orders.

This bureaucratic difficulty mirrors a wider challenge: in a more diverse society, where disability will be more common but shared identities may be less so, how do disability issues avoid becoming so diffuse that they disappear? In other words, how can the experience and recognition of disability become a spur for positive social change? We have argued that the answer lies in recognising disability without making it the sole factor by which people are defined – by their having a direct voice in the process of change, but sharing the practical responsibility for creating solutions.

In general people want the organisations through which they live their lives to be more responsive to their personal needs. Most people want greater democracy, but on their terms. In this sense, the politics of disablism presents an opportunity to teach wider society a lesson, to generate new tools for social innovation and to influence public attitudes through the process and not as an added extra.

Getting into the zone

We're not in a position to say what will work for individual disabled people, nor can we suggest which tools policy-makers should use when. Our perspective is slightly different. What we can do is suggest ways of overcoming the barriers that prevent change happening as quickly as it could. It is here that we can draw on an understanding of what makes trading zones effective and apply it to the three areas above. In each of these cases, all concerned should ask how they can create relationships that will lead to radical, sustainable change.

One of the important aspects of 'trading' is that you enter the zone with something to trade (resources, skills, experience) and leave with something you want. This section suggests what some of the important players might get out of more effective trading zones.

Flexibility

In the area of flexibility there is a need to develop an effective trading zone for personalised systems of work and support. This will bring together people with experience of large organisations, small organisations and the current support systems as well as disabled people who work and disabled people who don't. The idea would be to develop a template for work and support that benefits all those involved:

○ The benefit for government and service providers would be an understanding of the pressures that organisations feel as they become more flexible and adapt to disabled people's needs. What policies help? Which ones hinder? They would also be able to understand how support systems could be organised better to deliver more personalised support without extra resource implications.

○ The organisations involved should be able improve their performance by understanding better what action on their part would allow the disabled people who work for them to achieve their full potential and how they could encourage the disabled people who don't work to become part of their organisation.

O It is to be hoped that the disabled people would come away with a system more in tune with their needs.

Innovation

In the area of innovation there is a need to find more effective methods of upstream engagement. An effective trading zone would include those who 'do' innovation, those who manage the environment in which innovation takes place and disabled people who could contribute good ideas and their experience of what works and what doesn't:

O Architects, technology developers, product designers and systems engineers would learn new ways of working with disabled people, thus making their products and services more inclusive and giving them improved functionality.

O Managers and policy-makers would learn how there could be better incentives for upstream engagement in order to foster innovation and organisational success.

O Disabled people should end up with products, services and a built environment that meet their needs as well as an effective process for ongoing collaboration.

Communication

And when it comes to tackling disablism through communication there is a need to bring together people who can develop techniques for influencing public behaviour that go beyond the 'carrots, sticks and sermons' currently on offer:

O People from other equalities movements would gain new insights into emerging techniques for influencing public behaviour relevant to their own agenda.

O Authors, journalists, advertising creatives and other communicators would come away with a better

understanding of how to portray and communicate with
disabled people and the readership and market they
represent.

○   Policy-makers and disability campaigners would gain new
techniques for influencing the attitudes behind
discrimination that hold back the drive for equality.

○   Disabled people could eventually feel less like 'little green
men' as disablism becomes less acceptable.

Possible obstacles

These are just some of the people who should be involved in these
trading zones – meeting points between cultures and institutions – and
some of the benefits they might reap from the experience. It is also
important to realise that in some cases the benefits may not be so clear
and there may be other obstacles to getting involved. For example:

○   The financial barriers to disabled people collaborating
equally should not be underestimated. At the moment,
many aspects of life are more expensive for disabled
people and they are less likely to be in an economic
position to contribute their time, skills and experience
without compensation.

○   How and where people interact can also be a problem.
Disabled people require venues, materials and
communication that are accessible and non-intimidating;
in addition, an environment that fosters creativity would
benefit all those involved.

○   Some people will need to leave the chip on their shoulder
at the door. Others will need their confidence reinforced.
Creating equal communication should be a priority.

These barriers are significant but surmountable and if effective
trading zones can be created the prizes could be great.

Disablism is a major barrier to progress and it needs to come
crashing down. As our institutional landscape reacts and adapts to the

twenty-first century an opportunity exists to create a system that is better for all of us. We would do well to ensure that disabled people are at the centre of it. Without their involvement, reform will be paler, more piecemeal and less sustainable. Those at the forefront of change need to realise this.

Notes

1   M Oliver, *The Politics of Disablement* (Basingstoke: Macmillan, 1990).
2   L Barton, 'Sociology and disability: some emerging issues' in L Barton,
     Disability and Society: emerging issues and insights (Harlow: Pearson Education,
     1996).
3   The Prime Minister's Strategy Unit will publish a comprehensive review of
     statistics relating to the life chances of disabled people in June 2004.
4   Disability Rights Commission, *Disability Briefing* (London: DRC, Jan 2004),
     available at www.drc-gb.org.
5   Disability Rights Commission, *Young Disabled People Research* (London: DRC,
     Feb 2003), available at www.drc-gb.org.
6   Cabinet Office data and National Statistics 2004; for more details see
     www.diversity-whatworks.gov.uk/documents/22-04-04pressnotice.pdf.
7   DRC, *Disability Briefing*.
8   Disability Rights Commission, *The Web Access and Inclusion for Disabled People:
     a formal investigation* (London: Stationery Office, 2004).
9   Disability Rights Commission, *Overview of the Literature on Disability and
     Transport* (London: DRC, Nov 2003), available at www.drc-gb.org.
10   UCAS, available at www.ucas.ac.uk/figures/ucasdata/disability/.
11   Calvi, N, 'Paper Shame', *Disability Now*, April 2004.
12   Home Office, *Crime in England and Wales 2002/03* (London: Stationery Office,
     2003).
13   Disability Rights Commission, *Attitudes and Awareness Survey 2003* (London:
     DRC, 2003), available at www.drc-gb.org.
14   DRC, *Disability Briefing*.
15   I Christie, *An Inclusive Future?* (London: Demos, 1999).
16   For a history of Disabled Peoples' International see D Driedger, *The Last Civil
     Rights Movement: Disabled Peoples' International* (London: C Hurst & Co,
     1989).
17   J Chapman, *System Failure: how governments must learn to think differently*, 2nd
     edn (London: Demos, 2004).

18 T Bentley, 'Letting Go: complexity, individualism and the left', *Renewal* 10, no 1 (Winter 2002).

19 P Galison, *Image and Logic* (Chicago: Chicago University Press, 1997).

20 For more information about independent advocacy see W Lewington and C Clipson, *Advocating for Equality* (London: Scope, 2004).

21 P Galison, *Image and Logic.*

22 Ibid.

23 Zoe van Zuranenberg, quoted in D Chesterman and M Horne, *Local Authority? How to develop leadership for better public services* (London: Demos, 2002).

24 K Stanley and S Regan, *The Missing Million: supporting disabled people into work* (London: Institute for Public Policy Research, 2003).

25 R Layard, *Happiness: has social science a clue?* (London, London School of Economics, Lionel Robbins Memorial Lectures 2002/3, 2003).

26 T Bentley, *Learning Beyond the Classroom: education for a changing world* (London: Routledge, 1998).

27 P Tiihonen (ed), *Painspots in the Future of Work* (Finland: Committee for the Future, Government Institute for Economic Research, 2000).

28 J Morris, 'Social exclusion and young disabled people with high levels of support needs' in *Critical Social Policy* 21 no 2 (2001).

29 Stephen Ladyman MP, a minister in the Department of Health, in a speech given to the New Beginnings Symposium, 11 March 2004.

30 C Leadbeater, 'Open innovation in public services' in T Bentley and J Wilsdon (eds), *The Adaptive State: strategies for personalising the public realm* (London: Demos, 2003).

31 Demos interview with Simon Duffy, coordinator of In Control (March 2004).

32 'Wrap rage hitting the over-50s', BBC News online (4 Feb 2004), available at http://news.bbc.co.uk/1/hi/business/3456645.stm.

33 A report by the Social Exclusion Unit, *Making the Connections: final report on transport and social exclusion* (London: Office of the Deputy Prime Minister, Feb 2003).

34 Demos interview with Neil Crowther, Policy Manager, Disability Rights Commission (22 March 2004).

35 Also ex-Helen Hamlyn Research Associates.

36 'Wrap rage hitting the over-50s'.

37 Sensory Design Services, available at www.sds-uk.org/case-studies/bt/.

38 J Huber and P Skidmore, *The New Old: why the baby boomers won't be pensioned off* (London: Demos, 2003).

39 G Hamel, 'Innovation Now', *Fast Company*, no 65, 2002.

40 S Yates, 'Diversity, innovation and the future of Australian business', speech to the Department of Immigration and Multicultural Affairs Conference, 14 Nov 2000.

41 G Hamel, 'Innovation Now'.

42 Chapman, *System Failure.*

43 T Homer Dixon, *The Ingenuity Gap: facing the economic, environmental, and other challenges of an increasingly complex and unpredictable future* (New York: Knopf, 2000).

44   H Chesbrough, *Open Innovation* (Boston, Mass: Harvard Business School Press, 2003).

45   G Hamel, 'Innovation Now'.

46   B Lundvall, *Product Innovation and Economic Theory* (Aalborg: Aalborg University, 2004 forthcoming).

47   Employers' Forum on Disability, *Promoting Change: becoming a disability confident organization* (London: EFD, 2003).

48   Prime Minister's Strategy Unit, *Strategic Audit Paper: personal responsibility and behaviour change* (London: Cabinet Office, forthcoming).

49   Douglas Jay, *The Socialist Case* (London: Faber and Faber, 1938).

50   T Bentley, *It's Democracy, Stupid* (London: Demos, 2001).

51   Quoted in J Harkin, *Mobilisation* (London: Demos, 2003).

52   J Maxmin and S Zuboff *The Support Economy: why corporations are failing individuals and the next stage of capitalism* (London: Allen Lane, 2003).

53   VK Rangan, S Karim and SK Sandberg, 'Do better at doing good', *Harvard Business Review*, (May–June 1996).

54   M Castells, 'Why networks matter' in H McCarthy, P Miller and P Skidmore (eds), *Network Logic: who governs in a connected world?* (London: Demos, 2004).

55   P Miller, 'The rise of network campaigning' in H McCarthy, P Miller and P Skidmore (eds), *Network Logic: who governs in a connected world?* (London: Demos, 2004).

56   P Miller, *Open Policy: threats and opportunities in a wired world* (London: Forum for the Future, 2002).

DEMOS – Licence to Publish

THE WORK (AS DEFINED BELOW) IS PROVIDED UNDER THE TERMS OF THIS LICENCE ("LICENCE"). THE WORK IS PROTECTED BY COPYRIGHT AND/OR OTHER APPLICABLE LAW. ANY USE OF THE WORK OTHER THAN AS AUTHORIZED UNDER THIS LICENCE IS PROHIBITED. BY EXERCISING ANY RIGHTS TO THE WORK PROVIDED HERE, YOU ACCEPT AND AGREE TO BE BOUND BY THE TERMS OF THIS LICENCE. DEMOS GRANTS YOU THE RIGHTS CONTAINED HERE IN CONSIDERATION OF YOUR ACCEPTANCE OF SUCH TERMS AND CONDITIONS.

1. **Definitions**
   a **"Collective Work"** means a work, such as a periodical issue, anthology or encyclopedia, in which the Work in its entirety in unmodified form, along with a number of other contributions, constituting separate and independent works in themselves, are assembled into a collective whole. A work that constitutes a Collective Work will not be considered a Derivative Work (as defined below) for the purposes of this Licence.
   b **"Derivative Work"** means a work based upon the Work or upon the Work and other pre-existing works, such as a musical arrangement, dramatization, fictionalization, motion picture version, sound recording, art reproduction, abridgment, condensation, or any other form in which the Work may be recast, transformed, or adapted, except that a work that constitutes a Collective Work or a translation from English into another language will not be considered a Derivative Work for the purpose of this Licence.
   c **"Licensor"** means the individual or entity that offers the Work under the terms of this Licence.
   d **"Original Author"** means the individual or entity who created the Work.
   e **"Work"** means the copyrightable work of authorship offered under the terms of this Licence.
   f **"You"** means an individual or entity exercising rights under this Licence who has not previously violated the terms of this Licence with respect to the Work, or who has received express permission from DEMOS to exercise rights under this Licence despite a previous violation.
2. **Fair Use Rights.** Nothing in this licence is intended to reduce, limit, or restrict any rights arising from fair use, first sale or other limitations on the exclusive rights of the copyright owner under copyright law or other applicable laws.
3. **Licence Grant.** Subject to the terms and conditions of this Licence, Licensor hereby grants You a worldwide, royalty-free, non-exclusive, perpetual (for the duration of the applicable copyright) licence to exercise the rights in the Work as stated below:
   a to reproduce the Work, to incorporate the Work into one or more Collective Works, and to reproduce the Work as incorporated in the Collective Works;
   b to distribute copies or phonorecords of, display publicly, perform publicly, and perform publicly by means of a digital audio transmission the Work including as incorporated in Collective Works;
   The above rights may be exercised in all media and formats whether now known or hereafter devised. The above rights include the right to make such modifications as are technically necessary to exercise the rights in other media and formats. All rights not expressly granted by Licensor are hereby reserved.
4. **Restrictions.** The licence granted in Section 3 above is expressly made subject to and limited by the following restrictions:
   a You may distribute, publicly display, publicly perform, or publicly digitally perform the Work only under the terms of this Licence, and You must include a copy of, or the Uniform Resource Identifier for, this Licence with every copy or phonorecord of the Work You distribute, publicly display, publicly perform, or publicly digitally perform. You may not offer or impose any terms on the Work that alter or restrict the terms of this Licence or the recipients' exercise of the rights granted hereunder. You may not sublicense the Work. You must keep intact all notices that refer to this Licence and to the disclaimer of warranties. You may not distribute, publicly display, publicly perform, or publicly digitally perform the Work with any technological measures that control access or use of the Work in a manner inconsistent with the terms of this Licence Agreement. The above applies to the Work as incorporated in a Collective Work, but this does not require the Collective Work apart from the Work itself to be made subject to the terms of this Licence. If You create a Collective Work, upon notice from any Licencor You must, to the extent practicable, remove from the Collective Work any reference to such Licensor or the Original Author, as requested.
   b You may not exercise any of the rights granted to You in Section 3 above in any manner that is primarily intended for or directed toward commercial advantage or private monetary

compensation. The exchange of the Work for other copyrighted works by means of digital file-sharing or otherwise shall not be considered to be intended for or directed toward commercial advantage or private monetary compensation, provided there is no payment of any monetary compensation in connection with the exchange of copyrighted works.

c If you distribute, publicly display, publicly perform, or publicly digitally perform the Work or any Collective Works, You must keep intact all copyright notices for the Work and give the Original Author credit reasonable to the medium or means You are utilizing by conveying the name (or pseudonym if applicable) of the Original Author if supplied; the title of the Work if supplied. Such credit may be implemented in any reasonable manner; provided, however, that in the case of a Collective Work, at a minimum such credit will appear where any other comparable authorship credit appears and in a manner at least as prominent as such other comparable authorship credit.

5. Representations, Warranties and Disclaimer

  a By offering the Work for public release under this Licence, Licensor represents and warrants that, to the best of Licensor's knowledge after reasonable inquiry:

    i Licensor has secured all rights in the Work necessary to grant the licence rights hereunder and to permit the lawful exercise of the rights granted hereunder without You having any obligation to pay any royalties, compulsory licence fees, residuals or any other payments;

    ii The Work does not infringe the copyright, trademark, publicity rights, common law rights or any other right of any third party or constitute defamation, invasion of privacy or other tortious injury to any third party.

  b EXCEPT AS EXPRESSLY STATED IN THIS LICENCE OR OTHERWISE AGREED IN WRITING OR REQUIRED BY APPLICABLE LAW, THE WORK IS LICENCED ON AN "AS IS" BASIS, WITHOUT WARRANTIES OF ANY KIND, EITHER EXPRESS OR IMPLIED INCLUDING, WITHOUT LIMITATION, ANY WARRANTIES REGARDING THE CONTENTS OR ACCURACY OF THE WORK.

6. Limitation on Liability. EXCEPT TO THE EXTENT REQUIRED BY APPLICABLE LAW, AND EXCEPT FOR DAMAGES ARISING FROM LIABILITY TO A THIRD PARTY RESULTING FROM BREACH OF THE WARRANTIES IN SECTION 5, IN NO EVENT WILL LICENSOR BE LIABLE TO YOU ON ANY LEGAL THEORY FOR ANY SPECIAL, INCIDENTAL, CONSEQUENTIAL, PUNITIVE OR EXEMPLARY DAMAGES ARISING OUT OF THIS LICENCE OR THE USE OF THE WORK, EVEN IF LICENSOR HAS BEEN ADVISED OF THE POSSIBILITY OF SUCH DAMAGES.

7. Termination

  a This Licence and the rights granted hereunder will terminate automatically upon any breach by You of the terms of this Licence. Individuals or entities who have received Collective Works from You under this Licence, however, will not have their licences terminated provided such individuals or entities remain in full compliance with those licences. Sections 1, 2, 5, 6, 7, and 8 will survive any termination of this Licence.

  b Subject to the above terms and conditions, the licence granted here is perpetual (for the duration of the applicable copyright in the Work). Notwithstanding the above, Licensor reserves the right to release the Work under different licence terms or to stop distributing the Work at any time; provided, however that any such election will not serve to withdraw this Licence (or any other licence that has been, or is required to be, granted under the terms of this Licence), and this Licence will continue in full force and effect unless terminated as stated above.

8. Miscellaneous

  a Each time You distribute or publicly digitally perform the Work or a Collective Work, DEMOS offers to the recipient a licence to the Work on the same terms and conditions as the licence granted to You under this Licence.

  b If any provision of this Licence is invalid or unenforceable under applicable law, it shall not affect the validity or enforceability of the remainder of the terms of this Licence, and without further action by the parties to this agreement, such provision shall be reformed to the minimum extent necessary to make such provision valid and enforceable.

  c No term or provision of this Licence shall be deemed waived and no breach consented to unless such waiver or consent shall be in writing and signed by the party to be charged with such waiver or consent.

  d This Licence constitutes the entire agreement between the parties with respect to the Work licensed here. There are no understandings, agreements or representations with respect to the Work not specified here. Licensor shall not be bound by any additional provisions that may appear in any communication from You. This Licence may not be modified without the mutual written agreement of DEMOS and You.